MznLnx

Missing Links Exam Preps

Exam Prep for

Introduction to Management Science

Hillier & Hillier, 2nd Edition

The MznLnx Exam Prep is your link from the texbook and lecture to your exams.
The MznLnx Exam Preps are unauthorized and comprehensive reviews of your textbooks.

All material provided by MznLnx and Rico Publications (c) 2010
Textbook publishers and textbook authors do not particpate in or contribute to these reviews.

MznLnx

Rico
Publications

Exam Prep for Introduction to Management Science
2nd Edition
Hillier & Hillier

Publisher: Raymond Houge
Assistant Editor: Michael Rouger
Text and Cover Designer: Lisa Buckner
Marketing Manager: Sara Swagger
Project Manager, Editorial Production: Jerry Emerson
Art Director: Vernon Lowerui

Product Manager: Dave Mason
Editorial Assitant: Rachel Guzmanji
Pedagogy: Debra Long
Cover Image: Jim Reed/Getty Images
Text and Cover Printer: City Printing, Inc.
Compositor: Media Mix, Inc.

(c) 2010 Rico Publications

ALL RIGHTS RESERVED. No part of this work covered by the copyright may be reproduced or used in any form or by an means--graphic, electronic, or mechanical, including photocopying, recording, taping, Web distribution, information storage, and retrieval systems, or in any other manner--without the written permission of the publisher.

Printed in the United States
ISBN:

For more information about our products, contact us at:
Dave.Mason@RicoPublications.com

For permission to use material from this text or product, submit a request online to:
Dave.Mason@RicoPublications.com

Contents

CHAPTER 1
Introduction   1

CHAPTER 2
Linear Programming: Basic Concepts   8

CHAPTER 3
The Art of Modeling with Spreadsheets   18

CHAPTER 4
Linear Programming: Formulation and Applications   21

CHAPTER 5
What-If Analysis for Linear Programming   25

CHAPTER 6
Transportation and Assignment Problems   28

CHAPTER 7
Network Optimization Problems   33

CHAPTER 8
PERT/CPM Models for Project Management   36

CHAPTER 9
Integer Programming   43

CHAPTER 10
Nonlinear Programming   47

CHAPTER 11
Goal Programming   53

CHAPTER 12
Decision Analysis   56

CHAPTER 13
Forecasting   65

CHAPTER 14
Queueing Models   73

CHAPTER 15
Computer Simulation: Basic Concepts   81

CHAPTER 16
Computer Simulation with Crystal Ball   91

ANSWER KEY   104

TO THE STUDENT

COMPREHENSIVE

The *MznLnx* Exam Prep series is designed to help you pass your exams. Editors at MznLnx review your textbooks and then prepare these practice exams to help you master the textbook material. Unlike study guides, workbooks, and practice tests provided by the texbook publisher and textbook authors, *MznLnx* gives you **all** of the material in each chapter in exam form, not just samples, so you can be sure to nail your exam.

MECHANICAL

The MznLnx Exam Prep series creates exams that will help you learn the subject matter as well as test you on your understanding. Each question is designed to help you master the concept. Just working through the exams, you gain an understanding of the subject--its a simple mechanical process that produces success.

INTEGRATED STUDY GUIDE AND REVIEW

MznLnx is not just a set of exams designed to test you, its also a comprehensive review of the subject content. Each exam question is also a review of the concept, making sure that you will get the answer correct without having to go to other sources of material. You learn as you go! Its the easiest way to pass an exam.

HUMOR

Studying can be tedious and dry. MznLnx's instructional design includes moderate humor within the exam questions on occassion, to break the tedium and revitalize the brain

Chapter 1. Introduction

1. _____, is the discipline of using scientific research-based principles, strategies, and other analytical methods, such as mathematical modeling to improve any organization's ability to enact rational, meaningful business management decisions.
   a. Management science
   b. Cross ownership
   c. Trustee
   d. Workflow

2. _____ in the USA, Canada, South Africa and Australia, and operational research in Europe, is an interdisciplinary branch of applied mathematics and formal science that uses methods such as mathematical modeling, statistics, and algorithms to arrive at optimal or near optimal solutions to complex problems. It is typically concerned with optimizing the maxima (profit, assembly line performance, crop yield, bandwidth, etc) or minima (loss, risk, etc.) of some objective function.
   a. AAAI
   b. A Stake in the Outcome
   c. Operations research
   d. A4e

3. An unrelated, but similarly named method is the Nelder-Mead method or downhill _____ due to Nelder ' Mead (1965) and is a numerical method for optimizing many-dimensional unconstrained problems, belonging to the more general class of search algorithms.

   In both cases, the method uses the concept of a simplex, which is a polytope of N + 1 vertices in N dimensions: a line segment in one dimension, a triangle in two dimensions, a tetrahedron in three-dimensional space and so forth.

   A system of linear inequalities defines a polytope as a feasible region.
   a. 33 Strategies of War
   b. 1990 Clean Air Act
   c. 28-hour day
   d. Simplex method

4. A _____ is a professional who provides advice in a particular area of expertise such as management, accountancy, the environment, entertainment, technology, law , human resources, marketing, medicine, finance, economics, public affairs, communication, engineering, sound system design, graphic design, or waste management.

   A _____ is usually an expert or a professional in a specific field and has a wide knowledge of the subject matter. A _____ usually works for a consultancy firm or is self-employed, and engages with multiple and changing clients.

a. 28-hour day
b. 1990 Clean Air Act
c. 33 Strategies of War
d. Consultant

5. _____ can be regarded as an outcome of mental processes (cognitive process) leading to the selection of a course of action among several alternatives. Every _____ process produces a final choice. The output can be an action or an opinion of choice.
a. 33 Strategies of War
b. Decision making
c. 1990 Clean Air Act
d. 28-hour day

6. _____ of the learning curve effect and the closely related experience curve effect express the relationship between equations for experience and efficiency or between efficiency gains and investment in the effort. The experience of 'learning curves' was first observed by the 19th Century German psychologist Hermann Ebbinghaus according to the difficulty of memorizing varying numbers of verbal stimuli, and subsequent learning about the complex processes of learning are discussed in the

.

The rule used for representing the learning curve effect states that the more times a task has been performed, the less time will be required on each subsequent iteration.

a. Spatial Decision Support Systems
b. Models
c. Distribution
d. Point biserial correlation coefficient

7. _____ is a way of expressing knowledge or belief that an event will occur or has occurred. In mathematics the concept has been given an exact meaning in _____ theory, that is used extensively in such areas of study as mathematics, statistics, finance, gambling, science, and philosophy to draw conclusions about the likelihood of potential events and the underlying mechanics of complex systems.

The word _____ does not have a consistent direct definition.

a. Standard deviation
b. Probability
c. Time series analysis
d. Statistics

8. In probability theory and statistics, a _____ identifies either the probability of each value of an unidentified random variable (when the variable is discrete), or the probability of the value falling within a particular interval (when the variable is continuous.) The _____ describes the range of possible values that a random variable can attain and the probability that the value of the random variable is within any (measurable) subset of that range. The Normal distribution, often called the 'bell curve'

When the random variable takes values in the set of real numbers, the _____ is completely described by the cumulative distribution function, whose value at each real x is the probability that the random variable is smaller than or equal to x.

a. Median
b. Frequency distribution
c. Probability distribution
d. Statistically significant

9. _____ constitute a class of computer-based information systems including knowledge-based systems that support decision-making activities.

_____ are a specific class of computerized information systems that supports business and organizational decision-making activities. A properly-designed _____ is an interactive software-based system intended to help decision makers compile useful information from raw data, documents, personal knowledge, and/or business models to identify and solve problems and make decisions.

a. Spatial Decision Support Systems
b. 28-hour day
c. Decision support systems
d. 1990 Clean Air Act

10. _____ is one of the four elements of marketing mix. An organization or set of organizations (go-betweens) involved in the process of making a product or service available for use or consumption by a consumer or business user.

The other three parts of the marketing mix are product, pricing, and promotion.

a. Job creation programs
b. Missing completely at random
c. Matching theory
d. Distribution

11. _____ is an advertisement in which a particular product specifically mentions a competitor by name for the express purpose of showing why the competitor is inferior to the product naming it.

This should not be confused with parody advertisements, where a fictional product is being advertised for the purpose of poking fun at the particular advertisement, nor should it be confused with the use of a coined brand name for the purpose of comparing the product without actually naming an actual competitor. ('Wikipedia tastes better and is less filling than the Encyclopedia Galactica.')

In the 1980s, during what has been referred to as the cola wars, soft-drink manufacturer Pepsi ran a series of advertisements where people, caught on hidden camera, in a blind taste test, chose Pepsi over rival Coca-Cola.

a. 1990 Clean Air Act
b. 28-hour day
c. 33 Strategies of War
d. Comparative advertising

12. In economics, _____ are business expenses that are not dependent on the activities of the business They tend to be time-related, such as salaries or rents being paid per month. This is in contrast to variable costs, which are volume-related (and are paid per quantity.)

In management accounting, _____ are defined as expenses that do not change in proportion to the activity of a business, within the relevant period or scale of production.

a. Transaction cost
b. Cost allocation
c. Cost of quality
d. Fixed costs

13. In economics and finance, _____ is the change in total cost that arises when the quantity produced changes by one unit. It is the cost of producing one more unit of a good. Mathematically, the _____ function is expressed as the first derivative of the total cost (TC) function with respect to quantity (Q.)

a. Transaction cost
b. Variable cost
c. Cost overrun
d. Marginal cost

14. _____s are expenses that change in proportion to the activity of a business. In other words, _____ is the sum of marginal costs. It can also be considered normal costs.
    a. Cost overrun
    b. Cost accounting
    c. Fixed costs
    d. Variable cost

15. In economics, business, retail, and accounting, a _____ is the value of money that has been used up to produce something, and hence is not available for use anymore. In economics, a _____ is an alternative that is given up as a result of a decision. In business, the _____ may be one of acquisition, in which case the amount of money expended to acquire it is counted as _____.
    a. Cost overrun
    b. Cost
    c. Cost allocation
    d. Fixed costs

16. In economics ' business, specifically cost accounting, the _____ is the point at which cost or expenses and revenue are equal: there is no net loss or gain, and one has 'broken even'. A profit or a loss has not been made, although opportunity costs have been paid, and capital has received the risk-adjusted, expected return.

For example, if the business sells less than 200 tables each month, it will make a loss, if it sells more, it will be a profit.

   a. Virtuous circle
   b. Fixed asset turnover
   c. Defined benefit pension plan
   d. Break-even point

17. The function f is called, variously, an _____, cost function, energy function, or energy functional. A feasible solution that minimizes (or maximizes, if that is the goal) the _____ is called an optimal solution.

Generally, when the feasible region or the _____ of the problem does not present convexity, there may be several local minima and maxima, where a local minimum x^* is defined as a point for which there exists some $\delta > 0$ so that for all x such that

$$\|x - x^*\| > $$

the expression

$$f(x^*) > $$

holds; that is to say, on some region around x^* all of the function values are greater than or equal to the value at that point.

   a. Objective function
   b. A Stake in the Outcome
   c. AAAI
   d. A4e

18. 'Speaking generally, properties are those physical quantities which directly describe the physical attributes of the system; _____s are those combinations of the properties which suffice to determine the response of the system. Properties can have all sorts of dimensions, depending upon the system being considered; _____s are dimensionless, or have the dimension of time or its reciprocal.'

The term can also be used in engineering contexts, however, as it is typically used in the physical sciences.

When the terms formal _____ and actual _____ are used, they generally correspond with the definitions used in computer science.

   a. 1990 Clean Air Act
   b. 28-hour day
   c. 33 Strategies of War
   d. Parameter

19. _____ is the study of how the variation (uncertainty) in the output of a mathematical model can be apportioned, qualitatively or quantitatively, to different sources of variation in the input of a model.

In more general terms uncertainty and sensitivity analyses investigate the robustness of a study when the study includes some form of mathematical modelling. While uncertainty analysis studies the overall uncertainty in the conclusions of the study, _____ tries to identify what source of uncertainty weights more on the study's conclusions.

a. No-bid contract
b. Sensitivity analysis
c. Foreign ownership
d. Policies and procedures

20. _____ is a Fortune 500, American multinational corporation headquartered in Cincinnati, Ohio, that manufactures a wide range of consumer goods. As of 2008, P'G is the 8th largest corporation in the world by market capitalization and 14th largest US company by profit.
a. Maturity of Organizations and Business Excellence - The Four-Phase Model
b. Turnover
c. Procter ' Gamble Co.
d. STAR

Chapter 2. Linear Programming: Basic Concepts

1. In mathematics, _____ is a technique for optimization of a linear objective function, subject to linear equality and linear inequality constraints. Informally, _____ determines the way to achieve the best outcome (such as maximum profit or lowest cost) in a given mathematical model and given some list of requirements represented as linear equations.

More formally, given a polytope (for example, a polygon or a polyhedron), and a real-valued affine function

$$f(x_1, x_2, \ldots, x_n) = c_1 x_1 + c_2 x_2 + \cdots + c_n x_n + d$$

defined on this polytope, a _____ method will find a point in the polytope where this function has the smallest (or largest) value.

a. Slack variable
b. 1990 Clean Air Act
c. Linear programming
d. Linear programming relaxation

2. The Program (or Project) Evaluation and Review Technique, commonly abbreviated _____, is a model for project management designed to analyze and represent the tasks involved in completing a given project.

_____ is a method to analyze the involved tasks in completing a given project, specially the time needed to complete each task, and identifying the minimum time needed to complete the total project.

_____ was developed primarily to simplify the planning and scheduling of large and complex projects.

a. PERT
b. 33 Strategies of War
c. 28-hour day
d. 1990 Clean Air Act

3. _____ is a form of communication that typically attempts to persuade potential customers to purchase or to consume more of a particular brand of product or service. 'While now central to the contemporary global economy and the reproduction of global production networks, it is only quite recently that _____ has been more than a marginal influence on patterns of sales and production. The formation of modern _____ was intimately bound up with the emergence of new forms of monopoly capitalism around the end of the 19th century and beginning of the 20th century as one element in corporate strategies to create, organize and where possible control markets, especially for mass produced consumer goods.

a. A Stake in the Outcome
b. Advertising
c. AAAI
d. A4e

Chapter 2. Linear Programming: Basic Concepts

4. In economics, business, retail, and accounting, a _____ is the value of money that has been used up to produce something, and hence is not available for use anymore. In economics, a _____ is an alternative that is given up as a result of a decision. In business, the _____ may be one of acquisition, in which case the amount of money expended to acquire it is counted as _____.
   a. Cost allocation
   b. Fixed costs
   c. Cost overrun
   d. Cost

5. _____ is the process whereby companies use cost accounting to report or control the various costs of doing business.

   _____ generally describes the approaches and activities of managers in short run and long run planning and control decisions that increase value for customers and lower costs of products and services.

   a. Cost Management
   b. Genbutsu
   c. Missing completely at random
   d. Strict liability

6. _____ is the process of estimation in unknown situations. Prediction is a similar, but more general term. Both can refer to estimation of time series, cross-sectional or longitudinal data.
   a. 1990 Clean Air Act
   b. Forecasting
   c. 28-hour day
   d. 33 Strategies of War

7. In queueing theory, a _____ is used to approximate a real queueing situation or system, so the queueing behaviour can be analysed mathematically. _____s allow a number of useful steady state performance measures to be determined, including:

   - the average number in the queue, or the system,
   - the average time spent in the queue, or the system,
   - the statistical distribution of those numbers or times,
   - the probability the queue is full, or empty, and
   - the probability of finding the system in a particular state.

Chapter 2. Linear Programming: Basic Concepts

These performance measures are important as issues or problems caused by queueing situations are often related to customer dissatisfaction with service or may be the root cause of economic losses in a business. Analysis of the relevant _____s allows the cause of queueing issues to be identified and the impact of proposed changes to be assessed.

Queuing models can be represented using Kendall's notation:

A/B/S/K/N/Disc

where:

- A is the interarrival time distribution
- B is the service time distribution
- S is the number of servers
- K is the system capacity
- N is the calling population
- Disc is the service discipline assumed

Many times the last members are omitted, so the notation becomes A/B/S and it is assumed that K = ☒>, N = ☒> and Disc = FIFO.

Some standard notation for distributions (A or B) are:

- M for a Markovian (exponential) distribution
- E>κ for an Erlang distribution with >κ phases
- D for Degenerate (or Deterministic) distribution (constant)
- G for General distribution (arbitrary)
- PH for a Phase-type distribution

_____s are generally constructed to represent the steady state of a queueing system, that is, the typical, long run or average state of the system. As a consequence, these are stochastic models that represent the probability that a queueing system will be found in a particular configuration or state.

a. Girsanov theorem
b. Markov process
c. Queueing theory
d. Queueing model

Chapter 2. Linear Programming: Basic Concepts 11

8. _____ is one of the managerial functions like planning, organizing, staffing and directing. It is an important function because it helps to check the errors and to take the corrective action so that deviation from standards are minimized and stated goals of the organization are achieved in desired manner. According to modern concepts, _____ is a foreseeing action whereas earlier concept of _____ was used only when errors were detected. _____ in management means setting standards, measuring actual performance and taking corrective action.

 a. Schedule of reinforcement
 b. Control
 c. Turnover
 d. Decision tree pruning

9. _____ of the learning curve effect and the closely related experience curve effect express the relationship between equations for experience and efficiency or between efficiency gains and investment in the effort. The experience of 'learning curves' was first observed by the 19th Century German psychologist Hermann Ebbinghaus according to the difficulty of memorizing varying numbers of verbal stimuli, and subsequent learning about the complex processes of learning are discussed in the

.

The rule used for representing the learning curve effect states that the more times a task has been performed, the less time will be required on each subsequent iteration.

 a. Distribution
 b. Models
 c. Point biserial correlation coefficient
 d. Spatial Decision Support Systems

10. _____ is an integrated communications-based process through which individuals and communities discover that existing and newly-identified needs and wants may be satisfied by the products and services of others.

_____ is defined by the American _____ Association as the activity, set of institutions, and processes for creating, communicating, delivering, and exchanging offerings that have value for customers, clients, partners, and society at large. The term developed from the original meaning which referred literally to going to market, as in shopping, or going to a market to buy or sell goods or services.

 a. Market development
 b. Marketing
 c. Customer relationship management
 d. Disruptive technology

11. _____ is one of the four elements of marketing mix. An organization or set of organizations (go-betweens) involved in the process of making a product or service available for use or consumption by a consumer or business user.

The other three parts of the marketing mix are product, pricing, and promotion.

a. Matching theory
b. Missing completely at random
c. Job creation programs
d. Distribution

Chapter 2. Linear Programming: Basic Concepts

12. In microeconomics, industrial organization is the field which describes the behavior of firms in the marketplace with regard to production, pricing, employment and other decisions. _____ in this field range from classical issues such as opportunity cost to neoclassical concepts such as factors of production.

- Production theory basics
    - production efficiency
    - factors of production
    - total, average, and marginal product curves
    - marginal productivity
    - isoquants ' isocosts
    - the marginal rate of technical substitution
- Economic rent
    - classical factor rents
    - Paretian factor rents
- Production possibility frontier
    - what products are possible given a set of resources
    - the trade-off between producing one product rather than another
    - the marginal rate of transformation
- Production function
    - inputs
    - diminishing returns to inputs
    - the stages of production
    - shifts in a production function
- Cost theory
    - the different types of costs
        - opportunity cost
        - accounting cost or historical costs
        - transaction cost
        - sunk cost
        - marginal cost
    - the isocost line
- Cost-of-production theory of value
- Long-run cost and production functions
    - long-run average cost
    - long-run production function and efficiency
    - returns to scale and isoclines
    - minimum efficient scale
    - plant capacity
- Economies of density
- Economies of scale
    - the efficiency consequences of increasing or decreasing the level of production
- Economies of scope
    - the efficiency consequences of increasing or decreasing the number of different types of products produced, promoted, and distributed
- Optimum factor allocation
    - output elasticity of factor costs
    - marginal revenue product
    - marginal resource cost
- Pricing
    - various aspects of the pricing decision
- Transfer pricing
    - selling within a multi-divisional company
- Joint product pricing
    - price setting when two products are linked
- Price discrimination

- o different prices to different buyers
- o types of price discrimination
- o yield management
- Price skimming
    - o price discrimination over time
- Two part tariffs
    - o charging a price composed of two parts, usually an initial fee and an ongoing fee
- Price points
    - o the effects of a non-linear demand curve on pricing
- Cost-plus pricing
    - o a markup is applied to a cost term in order to calculate price
    - o cost-plus pricing with elasticity considerations
    - o cost plus pricing is often used along with break even analysis
- Rate of return pricing
    - o calculate price based on the required rate of return on investment, or rate of return on sales
- Profit maximization
    - o determining the optimum price and quantity
    - o the totals approach
    - o marginal approach of production

a. Markup
b. Price floor
c. Topics
d. Pricing

13. In economics, _____ is the process by which a firm determines the price and output level that returns the greatest profit. There are several approaches to this problem. The total revenue--total cost method relies on the fact that profit equals revenue minus cost, and the marginal revenue--marginal cost method is based on the fact that total profit in a perfectly competitive market reaches its maximum point where marginal revenue equals marginal cost.
    a. 1990 Clean Air Act
    b. Net profit margin
    c. Profit margin
    d. Profit maximization

14. In optimization (a branch of mathematics), a _____ is a member of a set of possible solutions to a given problem. A _____ does not have to be a likely or reasonable solution to the problem. The space of all _____s is called the feasible region, feasible set, search space, or solution space.
    a. 1990 Clean Air Act
    b. Candidate solution
    c. Gibbs state
    d. Hann function

15. The function f is called, variously, an _____, cost function, energy function, or energy functional. A feasible solution that minimizes (or maximizes, if that is the goal) the _____ is called an optimal solution.

Generally, when the feasible region or the _____ of the problem does not present convexity, there may be several local minima and maxima, where a local minimum x^* is defined as a point for which there exists some $>\delta > 0$ so that for all x such that

$$\boxed{x} >$$

the expression

$$\boxed{x} >$$

holds; that is to say, on some region around x^* all of the function values are greater than or equal to the value at that point.

Chapter 2. Linear Programming: Basic Concepts

a. AAAI
b. A Stake in the Outcome
c. A4e
d. Objective function

16. 'Speaking generally, properties are those physical quantities which directly describe the physical attributes of the system; _____s are those combinations of the properties which suffice to determine the response of the system. Properties can have all sorts of dimensions, depending upon the system being considered; _____s are dimensionless, or have the dimension of time or its reciprocal.'

The term can also be used in engineering contexts, however, as it is typically used in the physical sciences.

When the terms formal _____ and actual _____ are used, they generally correspond with the definitions used in computer science.

a. 28-hour day
b. 1990 Clean Air Act
c. 33 Strategies of War
d. Parameter

17. In optimization (a branch of mathematics), a candidate solution is a member of a set of possible solutions to a given problem. A candidate solution does not have to be a likely or reasonable solution to the problem. The space of all candidate solutions is called the _____, feasible set, search space, or solution space.

a. 1990 Clean Air Act
b. Gibbs state
c. Hann function
d. Feasible region

18. _____, is the discipline of using scientific research-based principles, strategies, and other analytical methods, such as mathematical modeling to improve any organization's ability to enact rational, meaningful business management decisions.

a. Cross ownership
b. Workflow
c. Trustee
d. Management Science

19. An _____ is a series of advertisement messages that share a single idea and theme which make up an integrated marketing communication (IMC.) _____s appear in different media across a specific time frame.

Chapter 2. Linear Programming: Basic Concepts

The critical part of making an _____ is determining a champion theme, as it sets the tone for the individual advertisements and other forms of marketing communications that will be used.

a. Advertising campaign
b. A4e
c. AAAI
d. A Stake in the Outcome

20. In economics, and cost accounting, _____ describes the total economic cost of production and is made up of variable costs, which vary according to the quantity of a good produced and include inputs such as labor and raw materials, plus fixed costs, which are independent of the quantity of a good produced and include inputs (capital) that cannot be varied in the short term, such as buildings and machinery. _____ in economics includes the total opportunity cost of each factor of production in addition to fixed and variable costs.

The rate at which _____ changes as the amount produced changes is called marginal cost.

a. 33 Strategies of War
b. 1990 Clean Air Act
c. 28-hour day
d. Total cost

21. _____ is a way of expressing knowledge or belief that an event will occur or has occurred. In mathematics the concept has been given an exact meaning in _____ theory, that is used extensively in such areas of study as mathematics, statistics, finance, gambling, science, and philosophy to draw conclusions about the likelihood of potential events and the underlying mechanics of complex systems.

The word _____ does not have a consistent direct definition.

a. Time series analysis
b. Statistics
c. Standard deviation
d. Probability

22. In probability theory and statistics, a _____ identifies either the probability of each value of an unidentified random variable (when the variable is discrete), or the probability of the value falling within a particular interval (when the variable is continuous.) The _____ describes the range of possible values that a random variable can attain and the probability that the value of the random variable is within any (measurable) subset of that range. The Normal distribution, often called the 'bell curve'

When the random variable takes values in the set of real numbers, the _____ is completely described by the cumulative distribution function, whose value at each real x is the probability that the random variable is smaller than or equal to x.

a. Probability distribution
b. Median
c. Frequency distribution
d. Statistically significant

23. _____ is an advertisement in which a particular product specifically mentions a competitor by name for the express purpose of showing why the competitor is inferior to the product naming it.

This should not be confused with parody advertisements, where a fictional product is being advertised for the purpose of poking fun at the particular advertisement, nor should it be confused with the use of a coined brand name for the purpose of comparing the product without actually naming an actual competitor. ('Wikipedia tastes better and is less filling than the Encyclopedia Galactica.')

In the 1980s, during what has been referred to as the cola wars, soft-drink manufacturer Pepsi ran a series of advertisements where people, caught on hidden camera, in a blind taste test, chose Pepsi over rival Coca-Cola.

a. 33 Strategies of War
b. 1990 Clean Air Act
c. Comparative advertising
d. 28-hour day

Chapter 3. The Art of Modeling with Spreadsheets

1. _____ refers to the movement of cash into or out of a business or financial product. It is usually measured during a specified, finite period of time. Measurement of _____ can be used

   - to determine a project's rate of return or value. The time of _____s into and out of projects are used as inputs in financial models such as internal rate of return, and net present value.
   - to determine problems with a business's liquidity. Being profitable does not necessarily mean being liquid. A company can fail because of a shortage of cash, even while profitable.
   - as an alternate measure of a business's profits when it is believed that accrual accounting concepts do not represent economic realities. For example, a company may be notionally profitable but generating little operational cash (as may be the case for a company that barters its products rather than selling for cash.) In such a case, the company may be deriving additional operating cash by issuing shares evaluating default risk, re-investment requirements, etc.

   _____ is a generic term used differently depending on the context. It may be defined by users for their own purposes.

   a. Cash flow
   b. Gross profit margin
   c. Gross profit
   d. Sweat equity

2. In decision theory and estimation theory, the _____ of an estimator, $\hat{\theta}$, of an unknown parameter of the distribution, θ, is the expected value of the loss function

$$R(\theta, \hat{\theta}) = \mathbb{E}_\theta L(\theta, \hat{\theta}) = \int L(\theta, \hat{\theta})\, dP_\theta.$$

where dP_θ is a probability measure parametrized by θ.

- For a scalar parameter θ and a quadratic loss function,

$$L(\theta, \hat{\theta}) = (\theta - \hat{\theta})^2$$

the _____ function becomes the mean squared error of the estimate,

$$R(\theta, \hat{\theta}) = E_\theta (\theta - \hat{\theta})^2$$

- In density estimation, the unknown parameter is probability density itself. The loss function is typically chosen to be a norm in an appropriate function space. For example, for L^2 norm,

$$L(f, \hat{f}) = \|f - \hat{f}\|_2^2$$

the _____ function becomes the mean integrated squared error

$$R(f, \hat{f}) = E\|f - \hat{f}\|^2$$

a. Risk
b. Linear model
c. Risk aversion
d. Financial modeling

3. The general definition of an _____ is an evaluation of a person, organization, system, process, project or product. _____s are performed to ascertain the validity and reliability of information; also to provide an assessment of a system's internal control. The goal of an _____ is to express an opinion on the person / organization/system (etc) in question, under evaluation based on work done on a test basis.
   a. Audit
   b. Audit committee
   c. A Stake in the Outcome
   d. Internal control

4. The function f is called, variously, an _____, cost function, energy function, or energy functional. A feasible solution that minimizes (or maximizes, if that is the goal) the _____ is called an optimal solution.

Generally, when the feasible region or the _____ of the problem does not present convexity, there may be several local minima and maxima, where a local minimum x^* is defined as a point for which there exists some $>\delta > 0$ so that for all x such that

$$\|x\| >$$

the expression

$$\|x\| >$$

holds; that is to say, on some region around x^* all of the function values are greater than or equal to the value at that point.

a. A Stake in the Outcome
b. AAAI
c. A4e
d. Objective function

5. In general, a _____ is an arrangement to provide people with an income when they are no longer earning a regular income from employment.

The terms retirement plan or superannuation refer to a _____ granted upon retirement. Retirement plans may be set up by employers, insurance companies, the government or other institutions such as employer associations or trade unions.

a. Pension insurance contract
b. Wage
c. Pension
d. State Compensation Insurance Fund

Chapter 4. Linear Programming: Formulation and Applications

1. In mathematics, _____ is a technique for optimization of a linear objective function, subject to linear equality and linear inequality constraints. Informally, _____ determines the way to achieve the best outcome (such as maximum profit or lowest cost) in a given mathematical model and given some list of requirements represented as linear equations.

More formally, given a polytope (for example, a polygon or a polyhedron), and a real-valued affine function

$$f(x_1, x_2, \ldots, x_n) = c_1 x_1 + c_2 x_2 + \cdots + c_n x_n + d$$

defined on this polytope, a _____ method will find a point in the polytope where this function has the smallest (or largest) value.

 a. 1990 Clean Air Act
 b. Linear programming
 c. Slack variable
 d. Linear programming relaxation

2. The 'business case for _____', theorizes that in a global marketplace, a company that employs a diverse workforce (both men and women, people of many generations, people from ethnically and racially diverse backgrounds etc.) is better able to understand the demographics of the marketplace it serves and is thus better equipped to thrive in that marketplace than a company that has a more limited range of employee demographics.

An additional corollary suggests that a company that supports the _____ of its workforce can also improve employee satisfaction, productivity and retention.

 a. Virtual team
 b. Kanban
 c. Trademark
 d. Diversity

3. _____ of the learning curve effect and the closely related experience curve effect express the relationship between equations for experience and efficiency or between efficiency gains and investment in the effort. The experience of 'learning curves' was first observed by the 19th Century German psychologist Hermann Ebbinghaus according to the difficulty of memorizing varying numbers of verbal stimuli, and subsequent learning about the complex processes of learning are discussed in the

.

The rule used for representing the learning curve effect states that the more times a task has been performed, the less time will be required on each subsequent iteration.

Chapter 4. Linear Programming: Formulation and Applications

a. Spatial Decision Support Systems
b. Distribution
c. Point biserial correlation coefficient
d. Models

4. _____ is the planning process used to determine whether a firm's long term investments such as new machinery, replacement machinery, new plants, new products, and research development projects are worth pursuing. It is budget for major capital, or investment, expenditures.

Many formal methods are used in _____, including the techniques such as

- Net present value
- Profitability index
- Internal rate of return
- Modified Internal Rate of Return
- Equivalent annuity

These methods use the incremental cash flows from each potential investment, or project. Techniques based on accounting earnings and accounting rules are sometimes used - though economists consider this to be improper - such as the accounting rate of return, and 'return on investment.' Simplified and hybrid methods are used as well, such as payback period and discounted payback period.

a. Restricted stock
b. Gross profit
c. Gross profit margin
d. Capital budgeting

5. In business and accounting, _____s are everything of value that is owned by a person or company. Any property or object of value that one possesses, usually considered as applicable to the payment of one's debts is considered an _____. Simplistically stated, _____s are things of value that can be readily converted into cash.

a. A Stake in the Outcome
b. AAAI
c. A4e
d. Asset

6. _____ is a financial mechanism in which a debtor obtains the right to delay payments to a creditor, for a defined period of time, in exchange for a charge or fee. Essentially, the party that owes money in the present purchases the right to delay the payment until some future date. The discount, or charge, is simply the difference between the original amount owed in the present and the amount that has to be paid in the future to settle the debt.

a. Financial modeling
b. Discounting
c. Ruin theory
d. Linear model

7. _____ or net present worth (NPW) is defined as the total present value (PV) of a time series of cash flows. It is a standard method for using the time value of money to appraise long-term projects. Used for capital budgeting, and widely throughout economics, it measures the excess or shortfall of cash flows, in present value terms, once financing charges are met.
   a. Discounted cash flow
   b. Net present value
   c. Present value
   d. 1990 Clean Air Act

8. _____ is the value on a given date of a future payment or series of future payments, discounted to reflect the time value of money and other factors such as investment risk. _____ calculations are widely used in business and economics to provide a means to compare cash flows at different times on a meaningful 'like to like' basis.

If offered a choice between $100 today or $100 in one year, everyone will choose $100 today.

   a. 1990 Clean Air Act
   b. Net present value
   c. Discounted cash flow
   d. Present value

9. _____ is one of the managerial functions like planning, organizing, staffing and directing. It is an important function because it helps to check the errors and to take the corrective action so that deviation from standards are minimized and stated goals of the organization are achieved in desired manner. According to modern concepts, _____ is a foreseeing action whereas earlier concept of _____ was used only when errors were detected. _____ in management means setting standards, measuring actual performance and taking corrective action.
   a. Turnover
   b. Schedule of reinforcement
   c. Decision tree pruning
   d. Control

Chapter 4. Linear Programming: Formulation and Applications

10. _____ is a form of communication that typically attempts to persuade potential customers to purchase or to consume more of a particular brand of product or service. 'While now central to the contemporary global economy and the reproduction of global production networks, it is only quite recently that _____ has been more than a marginal influence on patterns of sales and production. The formation of modern _____ was intimately bound up with the emergence of new forms of monopoly capitalism around the end of the 19th and beginning of the 20th century as one element in corporate strategies to create, organize and where possible control markets, especially for mass produced consumer goods.
   a. A4e
   b. AAAI
   c. A Stake in the Outcome
   d. Advertising

11. _____, is the discipline of using scientific research-based principles, strategies, and other analytical methods, such as mathematical modeling to improve any organization's ability to enact rational, meaningful business management decisions.
   a. Management science
   b. Trustee
   c. Cross ownership
   d. Workflow

12. _____ is possibly the most important step in the model building sequence. It is also one of the most overlooked. Often the validation of a model seems to consist of nothing more than quoting the R^2 statistic from the fit (which measures the fraction of the total variability in the response that is accounted for by the model.)
   a. 1990 Clean Air Act
   b. 28-hour day
   c. 33 Strategies of War
   d. Model validation

13. In economics, business, retail, and accounting, a _____ is the value of money that has been used up to produce something, and hence is not available for use anymore. In economics, a _____ is an alternative that is given up as a result of a decision. In business, the _____ may be one of acquisition, in which case the amount of money expended to acquire it is counted as _____.
   a. Cost overrun
   b. Cost allocation
   c. Cost
   d. Fixed costs

Chapter 5. What-If Analysis for Linear Programming

1. 'Speaking generally, properties are those physical quantities which directly describe the physical attributes of the system; _____s are those combinations of the properties which suffice to determine the response of the system. Properties can have all sorts of dimensions, depending upon the system being considered; _____s are dimensionless, or have the dimension of time or its reciprocal.'

    The term can also be used in engineering contexts, however, as it is typically used in the physical sciences.

    When the terms formal _____ and actual _____ are used, they generally correspond with the definitions used in computer science.

    a. 33 Strategies of War
    b. 1990 Clean Air Act
    c. 28-hour day
    d. Parameter

2. In economics, business, retail, and accounting, a _____ is the value of money that has been used up to produce something, and hence is not available for use anymore. In economics, a _____ is an alternative that is given up as a result of a decision. In business, the _____ may be one of acquisition, in which case the amount of money expended to acquire it is counted as _____.
    a. Fixed costs
    b. Cost overrun
    c. Cost
    d. Cost allocation

3. _____s are expenses that change in proportion to the activity of a business. In other words, _____ is the sum of marginal costs. It can also be considered normal costs.
    a. Variable cost
    b. Cost accounting
    c. Cost overrun
    d. Fixed costs

4. A _____ is typically described as a deliberate plan of action to guide decisions and achieve rational outcome(s.) However, the term may also be used to denote what is actually done, even though it is unplanned.

    The term may apply to government, private sector organizations and groups, and individuals.

a. 28-hour day
b. 33 Strategies of War
c. Policy
d. 1990 Clean Air Act

5. The function f is called, variously, an _____, cost function, energy function, or energy functional. A feasible solution that minimizes (or maximizes, if that is the goal) the _____ is called an optimal solution.

Generally, when the feasible region or the _____ of the problem does not present convexity, there may be several local minima and maxima, where a local minimum x^* is defined as a point for which there exists some $>\delta > 0$ so that for all x such that

the expression

holds; that is to say, on some region around x^* all of the function values are greater than or equal to the value at that point.

a. AAAI
b. A Stake in the Outcome
c. Objective function
d. A4e

6. _____ is the study of how the variation (uncertainty) in the output of a mathematical model can be apportioned, qualitatively or quantitatively, to different sources of variation in the input of a model.

In more general terms uncertainty and sensitivity analyses investigate the robustness of a study when the study includes some form of mathematical modelling. While uncertainty analysis studies the overall uncertainty in the conclusions of the study, _____ tries to identify what source of uncertainty weights more on the study's conclusions.

a. No-bid contract
b. Foreign ownership
c. Policies and procedures
d. Sensitivity analysis

7. In mathematics, _____ is a technique for optimization of a linear objective function, subject to linear equality and linear inequality constraints. Informally, _____ determines the way to achieve the best outcome (such as maximum profit or lowest cost) in a given mathematical model and given some list of requirements represented as linear equations.

More formally, given a polytope (for example, a polygon or a polyhedron), and a real-valued affine function

$$f(x_1, x_2, \ldots, x_n) = c_1 x_1 + c_2 x_2 + \cdots + c_n x_n + d$$

defined on this polytope, a _____ method will find a point in the polytope where this function has the smallest (or largest) value.

a. Linear programming relaxation
b. 1990 Clean Air Act
c. Slack variable
d. Linear Programming

8. _____ is one of the managerial functions like planning, organizing, staffing and directing. It is an important function because it helps to check the errors and to take the corrective action so that deviation from standards are minimized and stated goals of the organization are achieved in desired manner. According to modern concepts, _____ is a foreseeing action whereas earlier concept of _____ was used only when errors were detected. _____ in management means setting standards, measuring actual performance and taking corrective action.

a. Decision tree pruning
b. Turnover
c. Schedule of reinforcement
d. Control

Chapter 6. Transportation and Assignment Problems

1. In economics, _____ is the desire to own something and the ability to pay for it. The term _____ signifies the ability or the willingness to buy a particular commodity at a given point of time.

   a. 1990 Clean Air Act
   b. 33 Strategies of War
   c. 28-hour day
   d. Demand

2. In economics, business, retail, and accounting, a _____ is the value of money that has been used up to produce something, and hence is not available for use anymore. In economics, a _____ is an alternative that is given up as a result of a decision. In business, the _____ may be one of acquisition, in which case the amount of money expended to acquire it is counted as _____.

   a. Cost overrun
   b. Fixed costs
   c. Cost
   d. Cost allocation

3. In optimization (a branch of mathematics), a _____ is a member of a set of possible solutions to a given problem. A _____ does not have to be a likely or reasonable solution to the problem. The space of all _____s is called the feasible region, feasible set, search space, or solution space.

   a. 1990 Clean Air Act
   b. Gibbs state
   c. Hann function
   d. Candidate solution

4. 'Speaking generally, properties are those physical quantities which directly describe the physical attributes of the system; _____s are those combinations of the properties which suffice to determine the response of the system. Properties can have all sorts of dimensions, depending upon the system being considered; _____s are dimensionless, or have the dimension of time or its reciprocal.'

The term can also be used in engineering contexts, however, as it is typically used in the physical sciences.

When the terms formal _____ and actual _____ are used, they generally correspond with the definitions used in computer science.

   a. 28-hour day
   b. 1990 Clean Air Act
   c. Parameter
   d. 33 Strategies of War

Chapter 6. Transportation and Assignment Problems

5. _____ plant, and equipment, is a term used in accountancy for assets and property which cannot easily be converted into cash. This can be compared with current assets such as cash or bank accounts, which are described as liquid assets. In most cases, only tangible assets are referred to as fixed.
   a. 33 Strategies of War
   b. 28-hour day
   c. 1990 Clean Air Act
   d. Fixed asset

6. In mathematics, _____ is a technique for optimization of a linear objective function, subject to linear equality and linear inequality constraints. Informally, _____ determines the way to achieve the best outcome (such as maximum profit or lowest cost) in a given mathematical model and given some list of requirements represented as linear equations.

   More formally, given a polytope (for example, a polygon or a polyhedron), and a real-valued affine function

   $$f(x_1, x_2, \ldots, x_n) = c_1 x_1 + c_2 x_2 + \cdots + c_n x_n + d$$

   defined on this polytope, a _____ method will find a point in the polytope where this function has the smallest (or largest) value.

   a. Linear programming relaxation
   b. Slack variable
   c. 1990 Clean Air Act
   d. Linear programming

7. An unrelated, but similarly named method is the Nelder-Mead method or downhill _____ due to Nelder ' Mead (1965) and is a numerical method for optimizing many-dimensional unconstrained problems, belonging to the more general class of search algorithms.

   In both cases, the method uses the concept of a simplex, which is a polytope of N + 1 vertices in N dimensions: a line segment in one dimension, a triangle in two dimensions, a tetrahedron in three-dimensional space and so forth.

   A system of linear inequalities defines a polytope as a feasible region.
   a. 33 Strategies of War
   b. 28-hour day
   c. 1990 Clean Air Act
   d. Simplex method

Chapter 6. Transportation and Assignment Problems

8. _____ is a Fortune 500, American multinational corporation headquartered in Cincinnati, Ohio, that manufactures a wide range of consumer goods. As of 2008, P'G is the 8th largest corporation in the world by market capitalization and 14th largest US company by profit.
    a. Turnover
    b. STAR
    c. Maturity of Organizations and Business Excellence - The Four-Phase Model
    d. Procter ' Gamble Co.

9. The _____ is one of the fundamental combinatorial optimization problems in the branch of optimization or operations research in mathematics. It consists of finding a maximum weight matching in a weighted bipartite graph.

In its most general form, the problem is as follows:

   There are a number of agents and a number of tasks.

    a. A4e
    b. A Stake in the Outcome
    c. AAAI
    d. Assignment problem

10. _____ is one of the four elements of marketing mix. An organization or set of organizations (go-betweens) involved in the process of making a product or service available for use or consumption by a consumer or business user.

The other three parts of the marketing mix are product, pricing, and promotion.

    a. Job creation programs
    b. Missing completely at random
    c. Matching theory
    d. Distribution

11. _____ is the amount of time someone works beyond normal working hours. Normal hours may be determined in several ways:

    - by custom (what is considered healthy or reasonable by society),
    - by practices of a given trade or profession,
    - by legislation,
    - by agreement between employers and workers or their representatives.

Chapter 6. Transportation and Assignment Problems

Most nations have _____ laws designed to dissuade or prevent employers from forcing their employees to work excessively long hours. These laws may take into account other considerations than the humanitarian, such as increasing the overall level of employment in the economy. One common approach to regulating _____ is to require employers to pay workers at a higher hourly rate for _____ work.

a. Industrial relations
b. Organizational effectiveness
c. Organizational structure
d. Overtime

12. _____s are the recurring expenses which are related to the operation of a business -- or to the operation of a device, component, piece of equipment or facility.

For a commercial enterprise, _____s fall into two broad categories:

- fixed costs, which are the same whether the operation is closed or running at 100% capacity
- variable costs, which may increase depending on whether more production is done, and how it is done (producing 100 items of product might require 10 days of normal time or take 7 days if overtime is used. It may be more or less expensive to use overtime production depending on whether faster production means the product can be more profitable.)

Overhead costs for a business are the cost of resources used by an organization just to maintain its existence. Overhead costs are usually measured in monetary terms, but non-monetary overhead is possible in the form of time required to accomplish tasks.

Examples of overhead costs include:

- payment of rent on the office space a business occupies
- cost of electricity for the office lights
- some office personnel wages

Non-overhead costs are incremental costs, such as the cost of raw materials used in the goods a business sells.

In the case of a device, component, piece of equipment or facility (for the rest of this article, all of these items will be referred to in general as equipment), it is the regular, usual and customary recurring costs of operating the equipment.

Chapter 6. Transportation and Assignment Problems

a. Induction programme
b. Intangible assets
c. Industrial market segmentation
d. Operating cost

13. _____s are expenses that change in proportion to the activity of a business. In other words, _____ is the sum of marginal costs. It can also be considered normal costs.

a. Fixed costs
b. Variable cost
c. Cost overrun
d. Cost accounting

14. The _____ is a combinatorial optimization algorithm which solves the assignment problem in polynomial time and which anticipated later primal-dual methods. It was developed and published by Harold Kuhn in 1955, who gave the name '_____' because the algorithm was largely based on the earlier works of two Hungarian mathematicians: D>énes KÅ'nig and JenÅ' Egerv>áry.

James Munkres reviewed the algorithm in 1957 and observed that it is (strongly) polynomial.

a. 33 Strategies of War
b. Hungarian method
c. 1990 Clean Air Act
d. 28-hour day

Chapter 7. Network Optimization Problems

1. In mathematics, _____ is a technique for optimization of a linear objective function, subject to linear equality and linear inequality constraints. Informally, _____ determines the way to achieve the best outcome (such as maximum profit or lowest cost) in a given mathematical model and given some list of requirements represented as linear equations.

More formally, given a polytope (for example, a polygon or a polyhedron), and a real-valued affine function

$$f(x_1, x_2, \ldots, x_n) = c_1 x_1 + c_2 x_2 + \cdots + c_n x_n + d$$

defined on this polytope, a _____ method will find a point in the polytope where this function has the smallest (or largest) value.

a. Linear programming
b. Slack variable
c. 1990 Clean Air Act
d. Linear programming relaxation

2. _____, is the discipline of using scientific research-based principles, strategies, and other analytical methods, such as mathematical modeling to improve any organization's ability to enact rational, meaningful business management decisions.

a. Cross ownership
b. Workflow
c. Trustee
d. Management Science

3. In economics, _____ is the desire to own something and the ability to pay for it. The term _____ signifies the ability or the willingness to buy a particular commodity at a given point of time.

a. Demand
b. 28-hour day
c. 33 Strategies of War
d. 1990 Clean Air Act

4. In optimization (a branch of mathematics), a _____ is a member of a set of possible solutions to a given problem. A _____ does not have to be a likely or reasonable solution to the problem. The space of all _____s is called the feasible region, feasible set, search space, or solution space.

a. Gibbs state
b. Hann function
c. 1990 Clean Air Act
d. Candidate solution

Chapter 7. Network Optimization Problems

5. _____ plant, and equipment, is a term used in accountancy for assets and property which cannot easily be converted into cash. This can be compared with current assets such as cash or bank accounts, which are described as liquid assets. In most cases, only tangible assets are referred to as fixed.
   a. 33 Strategies of War
   b. 28-hour day
   c. 1990 Clean Air Act
   d. Fixed asset

6. An unrelated, but similarly named method is the Nelder-Mead method or downhill _____ due to Nelder ' Mead (1965) and is a numerical method for optimizing many-dimensional unconstrained problems, belonging to the more general class of search algorithms.

   In both cases, the method uses the concept of a simplex, which is a polytope of N + 1 vertices in N dimensions: a line segment in one dimension, a triangle in two dimensions, a tetrahedron in three-dimensional space and so forth.

   A system of linear inequalities defines a polytope as a feasible region.
   a. 33 Strategies of War
   b. Simplex method
   c. 1990 Clean Air Act
   d. 28-hour day

7. _____ refers to the movement of cash into or out of a business or financial product. It is usually measured during a specified, finite period of time. Measurement of _____ can be used

   - to determine a project's rate of return or value. The time of _____s into and out of projects are used as inputs in financial models such as internal rate of return, and net present value.
   - to determine problems with a business's liquidity. Being profitable does not necessarily mean being liquid. A company can fail because of a shortage of cash, even while profitable.
   - as an alternate measure of a business's profits when it is believed that accrual accounting concepts do not represent economic realities. For example, a company may be notionally profitable but generating little operational cash (as may be the case for a company that barters its products rather than selling for cash.) In such a case, the company may be deriving additional operating cash by issuing shares evaluating default risk, re-investment requirements, etc.

   _____ is a generic term used differently depending on the context. It may be defined by users for their own purposes.

a. Gross profit
b. Sweat equity
c. Gross profit margin
d. Cash flow

8. The _____ is a combinatorial optimization algorithm which solves the assignment problem in polynomial time and which anticipated later primal-dual methods. It was developed and published by Harold Kuhn in 1955, who gave the name '_____' because the algorithm was largely based on the earlier works of two Hungarian mathematicians: D>énes KÅ'nig and JenÅ' Egerv>áry.

James Munkres reviewed the algorithm in 1957 and observed that it is (strongly) polynomial.

a. 33 Strategies of War
b. 28-hour day
c. 1990 Clean Air Act
d. Hungarian method

Chapter 8. PERT/CPM Models for Project Management

1. The _____, is a mathematically based algorithm for scheduling a set of project activities. It is an important tool for effective project management.

It was developed in the 1950s by the Dupont Corporation at about the same time that General Dynamics and the US Navy were developing the Program Evaluation and Review Technique (PERT) Today, it is commonly used with all forms of projects, including construction, software development, research projects, product development, engineering, and plant maintenance, among others.

   a. 28-hour day
   b. Critical path method
   c. 1990 Clean Air Act
   d. 33 Strategies of War

2. The Program (or Project) Evaluation and Review Technique, commonly abbreviated _____, is a model for project management designed to analyze and represent the tasks involved in completing a given project.

_____ is a method to analyze the involved tasks in completing a given project, specially the time needed to complete each task, and identifying the minimum time needed to complete the total project.

_____ was developed primarily to simplify the planning and scheduling of large and complex projects.

   a. PERT
   b. 33 Strategies of War
   c. 1990 Clean Air Act
   d. 28-hour day

3. _____ refers to the movement of cash into or out of a business or financial product. It is usually measured during a specified, finite period of time. Measurement of _____ can be used

   - to determine a project's rate of return or value. The time of _____s into and out of projects are used as inputs in financial models such as internal rate of return, and net present value.
   - to determine problems with a business's liquidity. Being profitable does not necessarily mean being liquid. A company can fail because of a shortage of cash, even while profitable.
   - as an alternate measure of a business's profits when it is believed that accrual accounting concepts do not represent economic realities. For example, a company may be notionally profitable but generating little operational cash (as may be the case for a company that barters its products rather than selling for cash.) In such a case, the company may be deriving additional operating cash by issuing shares evaluating default risk, re-investment requirements, etc.

_____ is a generic term used differently depending on the context. It may be defined by users for their own purposes.

a. Cash flow
b. Gross profit margin
c. Gross profit
d. Sweat equity

4. _____ is the discipline of planning, organizing and managing resources to bring about the successful completion of specific project goals and objectives. It is often closely related to and sometimes conflated with Program management.

A project is a finite endeavor--having specific start and completion dates--undertaken to meet particular goals and objectives, usually to bring about beneficial change or added value.

a. Work package
b. Project engineer
c. Precedence diagram
d. Project management

5. A _____ is a graph (flow chart) depicting the sequence in which a project's terminal elements are to be completed by showing terminal elements and their dependencies.

The work breakdown structure or the product breakdown structure show the 'part-whole' relations. In contrast, the _____ shows the 'before-after' relations.

a. 28-hour day
b. 1990 Clean Air Act
c. 33 Strategies of War
d. Project network

6. A _____ is a type of bar chart that illustrates a project schedule. _____s illustrate the start and finish dates of the terminal elements and summary elements of a project. Terminal elements and summary elements comprise the work breakdown structure of the project.

a. 28-hour day
b. 33 Strategies of War
c. 1990 Clean Air Act
d. Gantt chart

Chapter 8. PERT/CPM Models for Project Management

7. In statistics, _____ is:

   - the arithmetic _____
   - the expected value of a random variable, which is also called the population _____.

It is sometimes stated that the '_____' _____s average. This is incorrect if '_____' is taken in the specific sense of 'arithmetic _____' as there are different types of averages: the _____, median, and mode. Other simple statistical analyses use measures of spread, such as range, interquartile range, or standard deviation. For a real-valued random variable X, the _____ is the expectation of X. Note that not every probability distribution has a defined _____; see the Cauchy distribution for an example.

   a. Mean
   b. Control chart
   c. Correlation
   d. Statistical inference

8. _____ is a way of expressing knowledge or belief that an event will occur or has occurred. In mathematics the concept has been given an exact meaning in _____ theory, that is used extensively in such areas of study as mathematics, statistics, finance, gambling, science, and philosophy to draw conclusions about the likelihood of potential events and the underlying mechanics of complex systems.

The word _____ does not have a consistent direct definition.

   a. Standard deviation
   b. Statistics
   c. Time series analysis
   d. Probability

9. In probability theory and statistics, a _____ identifies either the probability of each value of an unidentified random variable (when the variable is discrete), or the probability of the value falling within a particular interval (when the variable is continuous.) The _____ describes the range of possible values that a random variable can attain and the probability that the value of the random variable is within any (measurable) subset of that range. The Normal distribution, often called the 'bell curve'

When the random variable takes values in the set of real numbers, the _____ is completely described by the cumulative distribution function, whose value at each real x is the probability that the random variable is smaller than or equal to x.

a. Frequency distribution
b. Median
c. Statistically significant
d. Probability distribution

10. In mathematics, _____ are used in the study of chance and probability. They were developed to assist in the analysis of games of chance, stochastic events, and the results of scientific experiments by capturing only the mathematical properties necessary to answer probabilistic questions. Further formalizations have firmly grounded the entity in the theoretical domains of mathematics by making use of measure theory.

a. Time series
b. Median
c. Correlation
d. Random variables

11. _____ is one of the four elements of marketing mix. An organization or set of organizations (go-betweens) involved in the process of making a product or service available for use or consumption by a consumer or business user.

The other three parts of the marketing mix are product, pricing, and promotion.

a. Missing completely at random
b. Distribution
c. Job creation programs
d. Matching theory

12. In probability theory and statistics, the _____ or Gaussian distribution is a continuous probability distribution that describes data that clusters around a mean or average. The graph of the associated probability density function is bell-shaped, with a peak at the mean, and is known as the Gaussian function or bell curve.

The _____ can be used to describe, at least approximately, any variable that tends to cluster around the mean.

a. Normal distribution
b. Histogram
c. Generalized normal distribution
d. Heteroskedastic

Chapter 8. PERT/CPM Models for Project Management

13. In economics, business, retail, and accounting, a _____ is the value of money that has been used up to produce something, and hence is not available for use anymore. In economics, a _____ is an alternative that is given up as a result of a decision. In business, the _____ may be one of acquisition, in which case the amount of money expended to acquire it is counted as _____.
    a. Cost allocation
    b. Fixed costs
    c. Cost overrun
    d. Cost

14. In economics and finance, _____ is the change in total cost that arises when the quantity produced changes by one unit. It is the cost of producing one more unit of a good. Mathematically, the _____ function is expressed as the first derivative of the total cost (TC) function with respect to quantity (Q.)
    a. Cost overrun
    b. Transaction cost
    c. Variable cost
    d. Marginal cost

15. In business, overhead, _____ or overhead expense refers to an ongoing expense of operating a business. The term overhead is usually used to group expenses that are necessary to the continued functioning of the business, but do not directly generate profits.

    Overhead expenses are all costs on the income statement except for direct labor and direct materials.

    a. Intangible assets
    b. Interlocking directorate
    c. Overhead cost
    d. Industrial market segmentation

16. In mathematics, _____ is a technique for optimization of a linear objective function, subject to linear equality and linear inequality constraints. Informally, _____ determines the way to achieve the best outcome (such as maximum profit or lowest cost) in a given mathematical model and given some list of requirements represented as linear equations.

    More formally, given a polytope (for example, a polygon or a polyhedron), and a real-valued affine function

    $$f(x_1, x_2, \ldots, x_n) = c_1 x_1 + c_2 x_2 + \cdots + c_n x_n + d$$

    defined on this polytope, a _____ method will find a point in the polytope where this function has the smallest (or largest) value.

Chapter 8. PERT/CPM Models for Project Management

a. Linear programming
b. Slack variable
c. Linear programming relaxation
d. 1990 Clean Air Act

17. In project management, a _____ is a subset of a project that can be assigned to a specific party for execution. Because of the similarity, _____s are often misidentified as projects.

Similar to a work breakdown structure, a _____ is part of a Plan Breakdown Structure, representing a collection of work actions necessary to create a specific result.

a. Project engineer
b. Project manager
c. Project management office
d. Work package

18. _____ generally refers to a list of all planned expenses and revenues. It is a plan for saving and spending. A _____ is an important concept in microeconomics, which uses a _____ line to illustrate the trade-offs between two or more goods.
a. 1990 Clean Air Act
b. Budget
c. 33 Strategies of War
d. 28-hour day

19. _____ is the process of estimation in unknown situations. Prediction is a similar, but more general term. Both can refer to estimation of time series, cross-sectional or longitudinal data.
a. 28-hour day
b. 33 Strategies of War
c. 1990 Clean Air Act
d. Forecasting

20. _____ is defined as excess of actual cost over budget. _____ is also sometimes called 'cost escalation,' 'cost increase,' or 'budget overrun.' However, cost escalation and increases do not necessarily result in _____s if cost escalation is included in the budget.

_____ is common in infrastructure, building, and technology projects.

a. Transaction cost
b. Quality costs
c. Cost of quality
d. Cost overrun

21. _____ is used to assign the available resources in an economic way. It is part of resource management.

In strategic planning,is a plan for using available resources, for example human resources, especially in the near term, to achieve goals for the future.

a. 33 Strategies of War
b. 1990 Clean Air Act
c. 28-hour day
d. Resource allocation

22. _____ , also referred to simply as a 'public offering' or 'flotation,' is when a company issues common stock or shares to the public for the first time. They are often issued by smaller, younger companies seeking capital to expand, but can also be done by large privately-owned companies looking to become publicly traded.

In an _____ the issuer may obtain the assistance of an underwriting firm, which helps it determine what type of security to issue (common or preferred), best offering price and time to bring it to market.

a. Outsourcing
b. Occupational Safety and Health Administration
c. Unemployment insurance
d. Initial public offering

Chapter 9. Integer Programming

1. In mathematics, _____ is a technique for optimization of a linear objective function, subject to linear equality and linear inequality constraints. Informally, _____ determines the way to achieve the best outcome (such as maximum profit or lowest cost) in a given mathematical model and given some list of requirements represented as linear equations.

More formally, given a polytope (for example, a polygon or a polyhedron), and a real-valued affine function

$$f(x_1, x_2, \ldots, x_n) = c_1 x_1 + c_2 x_2 + \cdots + c_n x_n + d$$

defined on this polytope, a _____ method will find a point in the polytope where this function has the smallest (or largest) value.

a. 1990 Clean Air Act
b. Linear programming
c. Slack variable
d. Linear programming relaxation

2. _____, is the discipline of using scientific research-based principles, strategies, and other analytical methods, such as mathematical modeling to improve any organization's ability to enact rational, meaningful business management decisions.
a. Cross ownership
b. Trustee
c. Management Science
d. Workflow

3. In mathematics, the _____ of a 0-1 integer program is the problem that arises by replacing the constraint that each variable must be 0 or 1 by a weaker constraint, that each variable belong to the interval [0,1].

That is, for each constraint of the form

$$\boxed{x} >$$

of the original integer program, one instead uses a pair of linear constraints

$$\boxed{x} >$$

The resulting relaxation is a linear program, hence the name. This relaxation technique transforms an NP-hard optimization problem (integer programming) into a related problem that is solvable in polynomial time (linear programming); the solution to the relaxed linear program can be used to gain information about the solution to the original integer program.

Chapter 9. Integer Programming

a. Slack variable
b. 1990 Clean Air Act
c. Nonlinear programming
d. Linear programming relaxation

4. _____ of the learning curve effect and the closely related experience curve effect express the relationship between equations for experience and efficiency or between efficiency gains and investment in the effort. The experience of 'learning curves' was first observed by the 19th Century German psychologist Hermann Ebbinghaus according to the difficulty of memorizing varying numbers of verbal stimuli, and subsequent learning about the complex processes of learning are discussed in the

.

The rule used for representing the learning curve effect states that the more times a task has been performed, the less time will be required on each subsequent iteration.

a. Distribution
b. Models
c. Point biserial correlation coefficient
d. Spatial Decision Support Systems

5. _____ is the study of how the variation (uncertainty) in the output of a mathematical model can be apportioned, qualitatively or quantitatively, to different sources of variation in the input of a model .

In more general terms uncertainty and sensitivity analyses investigate the robustness of a study when the study includes some form of mathematical modelling. While uncertainty analysis studies the overall uncertainty in the conclusions of the study, _____ tries to identify what source of uncertainty weights more on the study's conclusions.

a. Foreign ownership
b. Policies and procedures
c. No-bid contract
d. Sensitivity analysis

6. _____ is one of the four elements of marketing mix. An organization or set of organizations (go-betweens) involved in the process of making a product or service available for use or consumption by a consumer or business user.

The other three parts of the marketing mix are product, pricing, and promotion.

Chapter 9. Integer Programming

a. Matching theory
b. Job creation programs
c. Missing completely at random
d. Distribution

7. A _____ is the system of organizations, people, technology, activities, information and resources involved in moving a product or service from supplier to customer. _____ activities transform natural resources, raw materials and components into a finished product that is delivered to the end customer. In sophisticated _____ systems, used products may re-enter the _____ at any point where residual value is recyclable.

a. Packaging
b. Wholesalers
c. Drop shipping
d. Supply chain

8. In business and accounting, _____s are everything of value that is owned by a person or company. Any property or object of value that one possesses, usually considered as applicable to the payment of one's debts is considered an _____. Simplistically stated, _____s are things of value that can be readily converted into cash.

a. AAAI
b. Asset
c. A Stake in the Outcome
d. A4e

9. The _____ is one of the fundamental combinatorial optimization problems in the branch of optimization or operations research in mathematics. It consists of finding a maximum weight matching in a weighted bipartite graph.

In its most general form, the problem is as follows:

There are a number of agents and a number of tasks.

a. AAAI
b. A4e
c. A Stake in the Outcome
d. Assignment problem

10. In finance and economics, _____ or divestiture is the reduction of some kind of asset for either financial or ethical objectives or sale of an existing business by a firm. A _____ is the opposite of an investment.

Chapter 9. Integer Programming

   a. 28-hour day
   b. 1990 Clean Air Act
   c. Divestment
   d. 33 Strategies of War

11. In probability theory, a probability distribution is called _____ if its cumulative distribution function is _____. This is equivalent to saying that for random variables X with the distribution in question, Pr[X = a] = 0 for all real numbers a, i.e.: the probability that X attains the value a is zero, for any number a. If the distribution of X is _____ then X is called a _____ random variable.
   a. Connectionist expert systems
   b. Continuous
   c. Pay Band
   d. Decision tree pruning

12. A _____ is a decision support tool that uses a tree-like graph or model of decisions and their possible consequences, including chance event outcomes, resource costs, and utility. _____s are commonly used in operations research, specifically in decision analysis, to help identify a strategy most likely to reach a goal. Another use of _____s is as a descriptive means for calculating conditional probabilities.
   a. 1990 Clean Air Act
   b. 33 Strategies of War
   c. Decision tree
   d. 28-hour day

Chapter 10. Nonlinear Programming

1. In statistics, given a (random) sample ▢> the most general form of _____ is formulated as

   ▢>

   where ▢> may be nonlinear functions.

   In matrix notation this model can be written as

   ▢>

   where Y is an n >× 1 column vector, X is an n >× (p + 1) matrix, >β is a (p + 1) >× 1 vector of (unobservable) parameters, and >ε is an n >× 1 vector of errors, which are uncorrelated random variables each with expected value 0 and variance >σ^2. Note that depending on the context the sample can be seen as fixed (observable), or random.

   a. Panjer recursion
   b. Risk tolerance
   c. Linear model
   d. Risk

2. In mathematics, _____ is the process of solving a system of equalities and inequalities, collectively termed constraints, over a set of unknown real variables, along with an objective function to be maximized or minimized, where some of the constraints or the objective function are nonlinear.

   A typical nonconvex problem is that of optimizing transportation costs by selection from a set of transportion methods, one or more of which exhibit economies of scale, with various connectivities and capacity constraints. An example would be petroleum product transport given a selection or combination of pipeline, rail tanker, road tanker, river barge, or coastal tankship.

   a. 1990 Clean Air Act
   b. Linear programming relaxation
   c. Slack variable
   d. Nonlinear programming

3. _____ of the learning curve effect and the closely related experience curve effect express the relationship between equations for experience and efficiency or between efficiency gains and investment in the effort. The experience of 'learning curves' was first observed by the 19th Century German psychologist Hermann Ebbinghaus according to the difficulty of memorizing varying numbers of verbal stimuli, and subsequent learning about the complex processes of learning are discussed in the

The rule used for representing the learning curve effect states that the more times a task has been performed, the less time will be required on each subsequent iteration.

a. Distribution
b. Point biserial correlation coefficient
c. Spatial Decision Support Systems
d. Models

4. In economics, business, retail, and accounting, a _____ is the value of money that has been used up to produce something, and hence is not available for use anymore. In economics, a _____ is an alternative that is given up as a result of a decision. In business, the _____ may be one of acquisition, in which case the amount of money expended to acquire it is counted as _____.

a. Fixed costs
b. Cost overrun
c. Cost allocation
d. Cost

5. In economics, _____ and economies of scale are related terms that describe what happens as the scale of production increases. They are different terms and should not be used interchangeably.

In production, _____ refers to changes in output subsequent to a proportional change in all inputs (where all inputs increase by a constant factor).

a. 33 Strategies of War
b. 1990 Clean Air Act
c. 28-hour day
d. Returns to scale

6. The _____ is a combinatorial optimization algorithm which solves the assignment problem in polynomial time and which anticipated later primal-dual methods. It was developed and published by Harold Kuhn in 1955, who gave the name '_____' because the algorithm was largely based on the earlier works of two Hungarian mathematicians: D>énes KÅ'nig and JenÅ' Egerv>áry.

James Munkres reviewed the algorithm in 1957 and observed that it is (strongly) polynomial.

Chapter 10. Nonlinear Programming

a. 28-hour day
b. 1990 Clean Air Act
c. 33 Strategies of War
d. Hungarian method

7. The _____ is the weighted-average most likely outcome in gambling, probability theory, economics or finance.

What Does _____ Mean? The average of a probability distribution of possible returns, calculated by using the following formula:

E(R)= Sum: probability (in scenario i) * the return (in scenario i)

How do you calculate the average of a probability distribution? As denoted by the above formula, simply take the probability of each possible return outcome and multiply it by the return outcome itself. For example, if you knew a given investment had a 50% chance of earning a 10% return, a 25% chance of earning 20% and a 25% chance of earning -10%, the _____ would be equal to 7.5%:

= (0.5) (0.1) + (0.25) (0.2) + (0.25) (-0.1) = 0.075 = 7.5%

Although this is what you expect the return to be, there is no guarantee that it will be the actual return.

a. Inflation rate
b. Open compensation plan
c. Expected gain
d. Expected return

8. _____ is a way of expressing knowledge or belief that an event will occur or has occurred. In mathematics the concept has been given an exact meaning in _____ theory, that is used extensively in such areas of study as mathematics, statistics, finance, gambling, science, and philosophy to draw conclusions about the likelihood of potential events and the underlying mechanics of complex systems.

The word _____ does not have a consistent direct definition.

a. Time series analysis
b. Standard deviation
c. Statistics
d. Probability

Chapter 10. Nonlinear Programming

9. In probability theory and statistics, a _____ identifies either the probability of each value of an unidentified random variable (when the variable is discrete), or the probability of the value falling within a particular interval (when the variable is continuous.) The _____ describes the range of possible values that a random variable can attain and the probability that the value of the random variable is within any (measurable) subset of that range. The Normal distribution, often called the 'bell curve'

When the random variable takes values in the set of real numbers, the _____ is completely described by the cumulative distribution function, whose value at each real x is the probability that the random variable is smaller than or equal to x.

a. Median
b. Statistically significant
c. Frequency distribution
d. Probability distribution

10. _____ is one of the four elements of marketing mix. An organization or set of organizations (go-betweens) involved in the process of making a product or service available for use or consumption by a consumer or business user.

The other three parts of the marketing mix are product, pricing, and promotion.

a. Missing completely at random
b. Matching theory
c. Job creation programs
d. Distribution

11. In decision theory and estimation theory, the _____ of an estimator, $\hat{\theta}$, of an unknown parameter of the distribution, θ, is the expected value of the loss function

$$R(\theta, \hat{\theta}) = \mathbb{E}_\theta L(\theta, \hat{\theta}) = \int L(\theta, \hat{\theta})\, dP_\theta.$$

where dP_θ is a probability measure parametrized by θ.

- For a scalar parameter θ and a quadratic loss function,

$$L(\theta, \hat{\theta}) = (\theta - \hat{\theta})^2$$

the _____ function becomes the mean squared error of the estimate,

$$R(\theta, \hat{\theta}) = E_\theta (\theta - \hat{\theta})^2$$

- In density estimation, the unknown parameter is probability density itself. The loss function is typically chosen to be a norm in an appropriate function space. For example, for L^2 norm,

$$L(f, \hat{f}) = \|f - \hat{f}\|_2^2$$

the _____ function becomes the mean integrated squared error

$$R(f, \hat{f}) = E\|f - \hat{f}\|^2$$

a. Risk aversion
b. Linear model
c. Risk
d. Financial modeling

12. _____ is the amount of time someone works beyond normal working hours. Normal hours may be determined in several ways:

- by custom (what is considered healthy or reasonable by society),
- by practices of a given trade or profession,
- by legislation,
- by agreement between employers and workers or their representatives.

Most nations have _____ laws designed to dissuade or prevent employers from forcing their employees to work excessively long hours. These laws may take into account other considerations than the humanitarian, such as increasing the overall level of employment in the economy. One common approach to regulating _____ is to require employers to pay workers at a higher hourly rate for _____ work.

a. Organizational effectiveness
b. Industrial relations
c. Overtime
d. Organizational structure

13. _____s are expenses that change in proportion to the activity of a business. In other words, _____ is the sum of marginal costs. It can also be considered normal costs.
    a. Variable cost
    b. Cost accounting
    c. Cost overrun
    d. Fixed costs

14. _____, is the discipline of using scientific research-based principles, strategies, and other analytical methods, such as mathematical modeling to improve any organization's ability to enact rational, meaningful business management decisions.
    a. Workflow
    b. Management Science
    c. Cross ownership
    d. Trustee

15. _____ is a Fortune 500, American multinational corporation headquartered in Cincinnati, Ohio, that manufactures a wide range of consumer goods. As of 2008, P'G is the 8th largest corporation in the world by market capitalization and 14th largest US company by profit.
    a. Turnover
    b. Maturity of Organizations and Business Excellence - The Four-Phase Model
    c. STAR
    d. Procter ' Gamble Co.

Chapter 11. Goal Programming

1. The function f is called, variously, an _____, cost function, energy function, or energy functional. A feasible solution that minimizes (or maximizes, if that is the goal) the _____ is called an optimal solution.

Generally, when the feasible region or the _____ of the problem does not present convexity, there may be several local minima and maxima, where a local minimum x^* is defined as a point for which there exists some $>\delta > 0$ so that for all x such that

$$\|x - x^*\| \geq$$

the expression

$$f(x) \geq f(x^*)$$

holds; that is to say, on some region around x^* all of the function values are greater than or equal to the value at that point.

 a. A Stake in the Outcome
 b. Objective function
 c. A4e
 d. AAAI

2. _____, is the discipline of using scientific research-based principles, strategies, and other analytical methods, such as mathematical modeling to improve any organization's ability to enact rational, meaningful business management decisions.
 a. Cross ownership
 b. Workflow
 c. Trustee
 d. Management science

3. In microeconomics, industrial organization is the field which describes the behavior of firms in the marketplace with regard to production, pricing, employment and other decisions. _____ in this field range from classical issues such as opportunity cost to neoclassical concepts such as factors of production.

- Production theory basics
    - production efficiency
    - factors of production
    - total, average, and marginal product curves
    - marginal productivity
    - isoquants ' isocosts
    - the marginal rate of technical substitution
- Economic rent
    - classical factor rents
    - Paretian factor rents
- Production possibility frontier
    - what products are possible given a set of resources
    - the trade-off between producing one product rather than another
    - the marginal rate of transformation
- Production function
    - inputs
    - diminishing returns to inputs
    - the stages of production
    - shifts in a production function
- Cost theory
    - the different types of costs
        - opportunity cost
        - accounting cost or historical costs
        - transaction cost
        - sunk cost
        - marginal cost
    - the isocost line
- Cost-of-production theory of value
- Long-run cost and production functions
    - long-run average cost
    - long-run production function and efficiency
    - returns to scale and isoclines
    - minimum efficient scale
    - plant capacity
- Economies of density
- Economies of scale
    - the efficiency consequences of increasing or decreasing the level of production
- Economies of scope
    - the efficiency consequences of increasing or decreasing the number of different types of products produced, promoted, and distributed
- Optimum factor allocation
    - output elasticity of factor costs
    - marginal revenue product
    - marginal resource cost
- Pricing
    - various aspects of the pricing decision
- Transfer pricing
    - selling within a multi-divisional company
- Joint product pricing
    - price setting when two products are linked
- Price discrimination

- - - different prices to different buyers
    - types of price discrimination
    - yield management
- Price skimming
  - price discrimination over time
- Two part tariffs
  - charging a price composed of two parts, usually an initial fee and an ongoing fee
- Price points
  - the effects of a non-linear demand curve on pricing
- Cost-plus pricing
  - a markup is applied to a cost term in order to calculate price
  - cost-plus pricing with elasticity considerations
  - cost plus pricing is often used along with break even analysis
- Rate of return pricing
  - calculate price based on the required rate of return on investment, or rate of return on sales
- Profit maximization
  - determining the optimum price and quantity
  - the totals approach
  - marginal approach of production

a. Price floor
b. Topics
c. Pricing
d. Markup

4. In project management, a _____ is a subset of a project that can be assigned to a specific party for execution. Because of the similarity, _____s are often misidentified as projects.

Similar to a work breakdown structure, a _____ is part of a Plan Breakdown Structure, representing a collection of work actions necessary to create a specific result.

a. Project manager
b. Project management office
c. Work package
d. Project engineer

Chapter 12. Decision Analysis

1. _____ is the discipline comprising the philosophy, theory, methodology, and professional practice necessary to address important decisions in a formal manner. _____ includes many procedures, methods, and tools for identifying, clearly representing, and formally assessing the important aspects of a decision situation, for prescribing the recommended course of action by applying the maximum expected utility action axiom to a well-formed representation of the decision, and for translating the formal representation of a decision and its corresponding recommendation into insight for the decision maker and other stakeholders.

The term _____ was coined in 1964 by Ronald A. Howard, who since then, as a professor at Stanford University, has been instrumental in developing much of the practice and professional application of _____.

   a. Nominal group technique
   b. Kepner-Tregoe
   c. Decision model
   d. Decision analysis

2. _____ can be regarded as an outcome of mental processes (cognitive process) leading to the selection of a course of action among several alternatives. Every _____ process produces a final choice. The output can be an action or an opinion of choice.
   a. 28-hour day
   b. 33 Strategies of War
   c. 1990 Clean Air Act
   d. Decision making

3. In Bayesian inference, a _____, often called simply the prior, is a probability distribution representing knowledge or belief about an unknown quantity a priori, that is, before any data have been observed P(A). The unknown quantity could be a parameter, hypothesis or latent variable.

The posterior probability is then the conditional probability taking the data into account P(A | B).

   a. 1990 Clean Air Act
   b. Bayesian probability
   c. Prior probability distribution
   d. Conjugate prior

4. A _____ is a decision support tool that uses a tree-like graph or model of decisions and their possible consequences, including chance event outcomes, resource costs, and utility. _____s are commonly used in operations research, specifically in decision analysis, to help identify a strategy most likely to reach a goal. Another use of _____s is as a descriptive means for calculating conditional probabilities.

Chapter 12. Decision Analysis 57

a. 33 Strategies of War
b. 28-hour day
c. Decision tree
d. 1990 Clean Air Act

5. _____ is the study of how the variation (uncertainty) in the output of a mathematical model can be apportioned, qualitatively or quantitatively, to different sources of variation in the input of a model .

In more general terms uncertainty and sensitivity analyses investigate the robustness of a study when the study includes some form of mathematical modelling. While uncertainty analysis studies the overall uncertainty in the conclusions of the study, _____ tries to identify what source of uncertainty weights more on the study's conclusions.

a. Sensitivity analysis
b. Policies and procedures
c. No-bid contract
d. Foreign ownership

6. In probability theory and statistics, the _____ of a random variable is the integral of the random variable with respect to its probability measure. For discrete random variables this is equivalent to the probability-weighted sum of the possible values, and for continuous random variables with a density function it is the probability density -weighted integral of the possible values.
a. Expected value
b. AAAI
c. A Stake in the Outcome
d. A4e

7. In decision theory, the _____ is the price that one would be willing to pay in order to gain access to perfect information.

The problem is modeled with a payoff matrix R_{ij} in which the row index i describes a choice that must be made by the payer, while the column index j describes a random variable that the payer does not yet have knowledge of, that has probability p_j of being in state j. If the payer is to choose i without knowing the value of j, the best choice is the one that maximizes the expected monetary value:

$$\text{EMV} = \max_i \sum_j p_j R_{ij}.$$

where

$$\sum_j p_j R_{ij}.$$

is the expected payoff for action i i.e. the expectation value, and

$$\text{EMV} = \max_i$$

is choosing the maximum of these expectations for all available actions.

   a. Expected value of perfect information
   b. Ulysses pact
   c. Analytic Network Process
   d. ELECTRE

8. In game theory, a game is said to have _____ if all players know all moves that have taken place.

Chess is an example of a game with _____ as each player can see all of the pieces on the board at all times. Other examples of perfect games include tic tac toe, irensei and go.

In microeconomics, a state of _____ is assumed in some models of perfect competition. That is, assuming that all agents are rational and have _____, they will choose the best products, and the market will reward those who make the best products with higher sales.

   a. Perfect information
   b. Global games
   c. Complete information
   d. Transferable utility

9. In the study of probability, given two random variables X and Y, the _____ of X and Y defines the probability of events defined in terms of both X and Y. In the case of only two random variables, this is called a bivariate distribution, but the concept generalizes to any number random variables, giving a multivariate distribution.

Chapter 12. Decision Analysis

The joint probability distribution of a pair of random variables is defined by the joint cumulative distribution function;

$$$$

Similarly, the _____ of a multivariate distribution is defined by the joint cumulative distribution function for the set of random variables.

For discrete random variables, the joint probability mass function is

$$$$

Since these are probabilities, we have

$$$$

Similarly for continuous random variables, the joint probability density function can be written as $f_{X,Y}(x, y)$ and this is

$$$$

where $f_{Y|X}(y|x)$ and $f_{X|Y}(x|y)$ give the conditional distributions of Y given X = x and of X given Y = y respectively, and $f_X(x)$ and $f_Y(y)$ give the marginal distributions for X and Y respectively.

 a. 1990 Clean Air Act
 b. 33 Strategies of War
 c. 28-hour day
 d. Joint distribution

10. In Bayesian statistics _____ of a random event or an uncertain proposition is the conditional probability that is assigned after the relevant evidence is taken into account.

Let us have a priori belief that the probability distribution function is $p(>\theta)$ and an observation X with the likelihood $p(X \mid >\theta)$, then the _____ is defined as . The _____ can be written in the memorable form as .

a. Location-scale family
b. Pareto Analysis
c. Posterior probability
d. Law of the iterated logarithm

11. _____ is a way of expressing knowledge or belief that an event will occur or has occurred. In mathematics the concept has been given an exact meaning in _____ theory, that is used extensively in such areas of study as mathematics, statistics, finance, gambling, science, and philosophy to draw conclusions about the likelihood of potential events and the underlying mechanics of complex systems.

The word _____ does not have a consistent direct definition.

a. Time series analysis
b. Standard deviation
c. Statistics
d. Probability

12. A _____ is typically described as a deliberate plan of action to guide decisions and achieve rational outcome(s.) However, the term may also be used to denote what is actually done, even though it is unplanned.

The term may apply to government, private sector organizations and groups, and individuals.

a. 28-hour day
b. 33 Strategies of War
c. 1990 Clean Air Act
d. Policy

13. In economics, business, retail, and accounting, a _____ is the value of money that has been used up to produce something, and hence is not available for use anymore. In economics, a _____ is an alternative that is given up as a result of a decision. In business, the _____ may be one of acquisition, in which case the amount of money expended to acquire it is counted as _____.

a. Cost allocation
b. Cost
c. Cost overrun
d. Fixed costs

Chapter 12. Decision Analysis

14. In economics, _____ is a measure of the relative satisfaction from consumption of various goods and services. Given this measure, one may speak meaningfully of increasing or decreasing _____, and thereby explain economic behavior in terms of attempts to increase one's _____. For illustrative purposes, changes in _____ are sometimes expressed in units called utils.
    a. Indirect utility function
    b. A Stake in the Outcome
    c. Ordinal utility
    d. Utility

15. In decision theory and estimation theory, the _____ of an estimator, $\hat{\theta}$, of an unknown parameter of the distribution, θ, is the expected value of the loss function

$$R(\theta, \hat{\theta}) = \mathbb{E}_\theta L(\theta, \hat{\theta}) = \int L(\theta, \hat{\theta}) \, dP_\theta.$$

where dP_θ is a probability measure parametrized by θ.

- For a scalar parameter θ and a quadratic loss function,

$$L(\theta, \hat{\theta}) = (\theta - \hat{\theta})^2$$

the _____ function becomes the mean squared error of the estimate,

$$R(\theta, \hat{\theta}) = E_\theta(\theta - \hat{\theta})^2$$

- In density estimation, the unknown parameter is probability density itself. The loss function is typically chosen to be a norm in an appropriate function space. For example, for L^2 norm,

$$L(f, \hat{f}) = \|f - \hat{f}\|_2^2$$

the _____ function becomes the mean integrated squared error

$$R(f, \hat{f}) = E\|f - \hat{f}\|^2$$

a. Risk
b. Risk aversion
c. Linear model
d. Financial modeling

16. _____ is a concept in economics, finance, and psychology related to the behaviour of consumers and investors under uncertainty. _____ is the reluctance of a person to accept a bargain with an uncertain payoff rather than another bargain with a more certain, but possibly lower, expected payoff. For example, a risk-averse investor might choose to put his or her money into a bank account with a low but guaranteed interest rate, rather than into a stock that is likely to have high returns, but also has a chance of becoming worthless.
a. Risk
b. Panjer recursion
c. Ruin theory
d. Risk aversion

17. In economics, _____ behavior is in between risk aversion and risk seeking. If offered either â,¬50 or a 50% chance of â,¬100, a risk averse person will take the â,¬50, a risk seeking person will take the 50% chance of â,¬100, and a _____ person would have no preference between the two options.

In finance, when pricing an asset, a common technique is to figure out the probability of a future cash flow, then to discount that cash flow at the risk free rate.

a. 1990 Clean Air Act
b. Taleb distribution
c. Market risk
d. Risk neutral

18. In economics, the _____ of a good or of a service is the utility of the specific use to which an agent would put a given increase in that good or service, or of the specific use that would be abandoned in response to a given decrease. In other words, _____ is the utility of the marginal use -- which, on the assumption of economic rationality, would be the least urgent use of the good or service, from the best feasible combination of actions in which its use is included. Under the mainstream assumptions, the _____ of a good or service is the posited quantified change in utility obtained by increasing or by decreasing use of that good or service.
a. 28-hour day
b. 33 Strategies of War
c. Marginal utility
d. 1990 Clean Air Act

Chapter 12. Decision Analysis 63

19. _____ plant, and equipment, is a term used in accountancy for assets and property which cannot easily be converted into cash. This can be compared with current assets such as cash or bank accounts, which are described as liquid assets. In most cases, only tangible assets are referred to as fixed.
 a. 28-hour day
 b. 33 Strategies of War
 c. 1990 Clean Air Act
 d. Fixed asset

20. A _____ is a list of the general tasks and responsibilities of a position. Typically, it also includes to whom the position reports, specifications such as the qualifications needed by the person in the job, salary range for the position, etc. A _____ is usually developed by conducting a job analysis, which includes examining the tasks and sequences of tasks necessary to perform the job.
 a. Recruitment Process Insourcing
 b. Recruitment
 c. Recruitment advertising
 d. Job description

21. _____ are a class of electronic meeting systems, a collaboration technology designed to support meetings and group work . _____ are distinct from computer supported cooperative work (CSCW) technologies as _____ are more focused on task support, whereas CSCW tools provide general communication support .

_____ were referred to as a Group Support System (GSS) or an electronic meeting system since they shared similar foundations.

 a. Group decision support systems
 b. 1990 Clean Air Act
 c. Hoshin Kanri
 d. Learning organization

22. An _____ is a compact graphical and mathematical representation of a decision situation. It is a generalization of a Bayesian network, in which not only probabilistic inference problems but also decision making problems can be modeled and solved.

_____ was first developed in mid-1970s within the decision analysis community with an intuitive semantic that is easy to understand.

a. Institutionalism in international relations
b. Expected value of perfect information
c. Ulysses pact
d. Influence diagram

23. _____ constitute a class of computer-based information systems including knowledge-based systems that support decision-making activities.

_____ are a specific class of computerized information systems that supports business and organizational decision-making activities. A properly-designed _____ is an interactive software-based system intended to help decision makers compile useful information from raw data, documents, personal knowledge, and/or business models to identify and solve problems and make decisions.

a. 28-hour day
b. 1990 Clean Air Act
c. Spatial Decision Support Systems
d. Decision support systems

24. _____ is an advertisement in which a particular product specifically mentions a competitor by name for the express purpose of showing why the competitor is inferior to the product naming it.

This should not be confused with parody advertisements, where a fictional product is being advertised for the purpose of poking fun at the particular advertisement, nor should it be confused with the use of a coined brand name for the purpose of comparing the product without actually naming an actual competitor. ('Wikipedia tastes better and is less filling than the Encyclopedia Galactica.')

In the 1980s, during what has been referred to as the cola wars, soft-drink manufacturer Pepsi ran a series of advertisements where people, caught on hidden camera, in a blind taste test, chose Pepsi over rival Coca-Cola.

a. 1990 Clean Air Act
b. 33 Strategies of War
c. 28-hour day
d. Comparative advertising

Chapter 13. Forecasting

1. In economics, _____ is the desire to own something and the ability to pay for it. The term _____ signifies the ability or the willingness to buy a particular commodity at a given point of time.
   a. Demand
   b. 33 Strategies of War
   c. 1990 Clean Air Act
   d. 28-hour day

2. _____ is the process of estimation in unknown situations. Prediction is a similar, but more general term. Both can refer to estimation of time series, cross-sectional or longitudinal data.
   a. 33 Strategies of War
   b. 28-hour day
   c. 1990 Clean Air Act
   d. Forecasting

3. _____, is the discipline of using scientific research-based principles, strategies, and other analytical methods, such as mathematical modeling to improve any organization's ability to enact rational, meaningful business management decisions.
   a. Trustee
   b. Cross ownership
   c. Management science
   d. Workflow

4. _____ generally refers to a list of all planned expenses and revenues. It is a plan for saving and spending. A _____ is an important concept in microeconomics, which uses a _____ line to illustrate the trade-offs between two or more goods.
   a. Budget
   b. 33 Strategies of War
   c. 1990 Clean Air Act
   d. 28-hour day

5. _____s are statistical models used in econometrics. An _____ specifies the statistical relationship that is believed to hold between the various economic quantities pertaining a particular economic phenomena under study. An _____ can be derived from a deterministic economic model by allowing for uncertainty or from an economic model which itself is stochastic.

Chapter 13. Forecasting

    a. AAAI
    b. A4e
    c. A Stake in the Outcome
    d. Econometric model

6. _____ occurs when a person is available to work and seeking work but currently without work. The prevalence of _____ is usually measured using the _____ rate, which is defined as the percentage of those in the labor force who are unemployed. The _____ rate is also used in economic studies and economic indexes such as the United States' Conference Board's Index of Leading Indicators as a measure of the state of the macroeconomics.

    a. Unemployment Convention, 1919
    b. Unemployment
    c. Outplacement
    d. Employment-to-population ratio

7. Wisconsin originated the idea of _____ in the U.S. in 1932. In the United States, there are 50 state _____ programs plus one each in the District of Columbia and Puerto Rico. Through the Social Security Act of 1935, the Federal Government of the United States effectively coerced the individual states into adopting _____ plans.

    a. Unemployment Provision Convention, 1934
    b. Unemployment benefits
    c. Unemployment
    d. Unemployment insurance

8. _____ of the learning curve effect and the closely related experience curve effect express the relationship between equations for experience and efficiency or between efficiency gains and investment in the effort. The experience of 'learning curves' was first observed by the 19th Century German psychologist Hermann Ebbinghaus according to the difficulty of memorizing varying numbers of verbal stimuli, and subsequent learning about the complex processes of learning are discussed in the

.

The rule used for representing the learning curve effect states that the more times a task has been performed, the less time will be required on each subsequent iteration.

    a. Point biserial correlation coefficient
    b. Models
    c. Distribution
    d. Spatial Decision Support Systems

Chapter 13. Forecasting

9. _____ is an advertisement in which a particular product specifically mentions a competitor by name for the express purpose of showing why the competitor is inferior to the product naming it.

This should not be confused with parody advertisements, where a fictional product is being advertised for the purpose of poking fun at the particular advertisement, nor should it be confused with the use of a coined brand name for the purpose of comparing the product without actually naming an actual competitor. ('Wikipedia tastes better and is less filling than the Encyclopedia Galactica.')

In the 1980s, during what has been referred to as the cola wars, soft-drink manufacturer Pepsi ran a series of advertisements where people, caught on hidden camera, in a blind taste test, chose Pepsi over rival Coca-Cola.

   a. 28-hour day
   b. 33 Strategies of War
   c. Comparative advertising
   d. 1990 Clean Air Act

10. The term '_____' refers to the concept of collecting information and attempting to spot a pattern in the information. In some fields of study, the term '_____' has more formally-defined meanings.

In project management _____ is a mathematical technique that uses historical results to predict future outcome.

   a. Trend analysis
   b. Stepwise regression
   c. Least squares
   d. Regression analysis

11. A _____ is a commercial building for storage of goods. _____s are used by manufacturers, importers, exporters, wholesalers, transport businesses, customs, etc. They are usually large plain buildings in industrial areas of cities and towns.
   a. Warehouse
   b. 33 Strategies of War
   c. 1990 Clean Air Act
   d. 28-hour day

12. In statistics, _____ is:

- the arithmetic _____
- the expected value of a random variable, which is also called the population _____.

It is sometimes stated that the '_____' _____s average. This is incorrect if '_____' is taken in the specific sense of 'arithmetic _____' as there are different types of averages: the _____, median, and mode. Other simple statistical analyses use measures of spread, such as range, interquartile range, or standard deviation. For a real-valued random variable X, the _____ is the expectation of X. Note that not every probability distribution has a defined _____; see the Cauchy distribution for an example.

a. Correlation
b. Statistical inference
c. Control chart
d. Mean

13. The _____ or simply average deviation of a data set is the average of the absolute deviations and is a summary statistic of statistical dispersion or variability. It is also called the mean absolute deviation, but this is easily confused with the median absolute deviation.

The average absolute deviation of a set {$x_1, x_2, ..., x_n$} is

The choice of measure of central tendency, m(X), has a marked effect on the value of the average deviation.

a. A Stake in the Outcome
b. A4e
c. AAAI
d. Average absolute deviation,

14. In statistics, the _____ of an estimator is one of many ways to quantify the amount by which an estimator differs from the true value of the quantity being estimated. As a loss function, _____ is called squared error loss. _____ measures the average of the square of the 'error.' The error is the amount by which the estimator differs from the quantity to be estimated.

Chapter 13. Forecasting

a. 28-hour day
b. 33 Strategies of War
c. 1990 Clean Air Act
d. Mean squared error

15. In statistics, _____ is a technique that can be applied to time series data, either to produce smoothed data for presentation, or to make forecasts. The time series data themselves are a sequence of observations. The observed phenomenon may be an essentially random process, or it may be an orderly, but noisy, process.

   a. A Stake in the Outcome
   b. A4e
   c. AAAI
   d. Exponential smoothing

16. The term _____ usually refers to a weighted arithmetic mean, but weighted versions of other means can also be calculated, such as the weighted geometric mean and the weighted harmonic mean.

Given two school classes, one with 20 students, and one with 30 students, the grades in each class on a test were:

   Morning class = 62, 67, 71, 74, 76, 77, 78, 79, 79, 80, 80, 81, 81, 82, 83, 84, 86, 89, 93, 98

   Afternoon class = 81, 82, 83, 84, 85, 86, 87, 87, 88, 88, 89, 89, 89, 90, 90, 90, 90, 91, 91, 91, 92, 92, 93, 93, 94, 95, 96, 97, 98, 99

The straight average for the morning class is 80 and the straight average of the afternoon class is 90. The straight average of 80 and 90 is 85, the mean of the two class means.

   a. 33 Strategies of War
   b. 1990 Clean Air Act
   c. 28-hour day
   d. Weighted average

17. In statistics and image processing, to smooth a data set is to create an approximating function that attempts to capture important patterns in the data, while leaving out noise or other fine-scale structures/rapid phenomena. Many different algorithms are used in _____. One of the most common algorithms is the 'moving average', often used to try to capture important trends in repeated statistical surveys.

a. 1990 Clean Air Act
b. Smoothing
c. 28-hour day
d. 33 Strategies of War

18. In statistics, a _____ rolling mean or running average, is a type of finite impulse response filter used to analyze a set of data points by creating a series of averages of different subsets of the full data set. A _____ is not a single number, but it is a set of numbers, each of which is the average of the corresponding subset of a larger set of data points. A _____ may also use unequal weights for each data value in the subset to emphasize particular values in the subset.

a. Homoscedastic
b. Time series analysis
c. Moving Average
d. Standard deviation

19. _____ is a way of expressing knowledge or belief that an event will occur or has occurred. In mathematics the concept has been given an exact meaning in _____ theory, that is used extensively in such areas of study as mathematics, statistics, finance, gambling, science, and philosophy to draw conclusions about the likelihood of potential events and the underlying mechanics of complex systems.

The word _____ does not have a consistent direct definition.

a. Time series analysis
b. Probability
c. Standard deviation
d. Statistics

20. In probability theory and statistics, a _____ identifies either the probability of each value of an unidentified random variable (when the variable is discrete), or the probability of the value falling within a particular interval (when the variable is continuous.) The _____ describes the range of possible values that a random variable can attain and the probability that the value of the random variable is within any (measurable) subset of that range. The Normal distribution, often called the 'bell curve'

When the random variable takes values in the set of real numbers, the _____ is completely described by the cumulative distribution function, whose value at each real x is the probability that the random variable is smaller than or equal to x.

a. Median
b. Frequency distribution
c. Probability distribution
d. Statistically significant

21. In mathematics, _____ are used in the study of chance and probability. They were developed to assist in the analysis of games of chance, stochastic events, and the results of scientific experiments by capturing only the mathematical properties necessary to answer probabilistic questions. Further formalizations have firmly grounded the entity in the theoretical domains of mathematics by making use of measure theory.

   a. Correlation
   b. Time series
   c. Median
   d. Random variables

22. _____ is one of the four elements of marketing mix. An organization or set of organizations (go-betweens) involved in the process of making a product or service available for use or consumption by a consumer or business user.

The other three parts of the marketing mix are product, pricing, and promotion.

   a. Distribution
   b. Matching theory
   c. Job creation programs
   d. Missing completely at random

23. The terms '_____' and 'independent variable' are used in similar but subtly different ways in mathematics and statistics as part of the standard terminology in those subjects. They are used to distinguish between two types of quantities being considered, separating them into those available at the start of a process and those being created by it, where the latter (_____s) are dependent on the former (independent variables.)

The independent variable is typically the variable being manipulated or changed and the _____ is the observed result of the independent variable being manipulated.

   a. 1990 Clean Air Act
   b. Dependent variable
   c. 28-hour day
   d. Taguchi methods

24. In statistics, _____ is used for two things:

- to construct a simple formula that will predict a value or values for a variable given the value of another variable.
- to test whether and how a given variable is related to another variable or variables.

_____ is a form of regression analysis in which the relationship between one or more independent variables and another variable, called the dependent variable, is modelled by a least squares function, called a _____ equation. This function is a linear combination of one or more model parameters, called regression coefficients. A _____ equation with one independent variable represents a straight line when the predicted value (i.e. the dependent variable from the regression equation) is plotted against the independent variable: this is called a simple _____. However, note that 'linear' does not refer to this straight line, but rather to the way in which the regression coefficients occur in the regression equation.

a. Clinical decision support systems
b. Continuous
c. Linear regression
d. Strict liability

25. The method of _____ is used to approximately solve overdetermined systems, i.e. systems of equations in which there are more equations than unknowns. _____ is often applied in statistical contexts, particularly regression analysis.

_____ can be interpreted as a method of fitting data.

a. Regression analysis
b. Stepwise regression
c. Trend analysis
d. Least squares

26. The _____ is a systematic, interactive forecasting method which relies on a panel of independent experts. The carefully selected experts answer questionnaires in two or more rounds. After each round, a facilitator provides an anonymous summary of the experts' forecasts from the previous round as well as the reasons they provided for their judgments.

a. Quality function deployment
b. Hoshin Kanri
c. Learning organization
d. Delphi method

Chapter 14. Queueing Models

1. In queueing theory, a _____ is used to approximate a real queueing situation or system, so the queueing behaviour can be analysed mathematically. _____s allow a number of useful steady state performance measures to be determined, including:

   - the average number in the queue, or the system,
   - the average time spent in the queue, or the system,
   - the statistical distribution of those numbers or times,
   - the probability the queue is full, or empty, and
   - the probability of finding the system in a particular state.

   These performance measures are important as issues or problems caused by queueing situations are often related to customer dissatisfaction with service or may be the root cause of economic losses in a business. Analysis of the relevant _____s allows the cause of queueing issues to be identified and the impact of proposed changes to be assessed.

   Queuing models can be represented using Kendall's notation:

   A/B/S/K/N/Disc

   where:

   - A is the interarrival time distribution
   - B is the service time distribution
   - S is the number of servers
   - K is the system capacity
   - N is the calling population
   - Disc is the service discipline assumed

   Many times the last members are omitted, so the notation becomes A/B/S and it is assumed that K = ☒>, N = ☒> and Disc = FIFO.

   Some standard notation for distributions (A or B) are:

   - M for a Markovian (exponential) distribution
   - E>κ for an Erlang distribution with >κ phases
   - D for Degenerate (or Deterministic) distribution (constant)
   - G for General distribution (arbitrary)
   - PH for a Phase-type distribution

   _____s are generally constructed to represent the steady state of a queueing system, that is, the typical, long run or average state of the system. As a consequence, these are stochastic models that represent the probability that a queueing system will be found in a particular configuration or state.

a. Queueing model
b. Queueing theory
c. Girsanov theorem
d. Markov process

2. _____ of the learning curve effect and the closely related experience curve effect express the relationship between equations for experience and efficiency or between efficiency gains and investment in the effort. The experience of 'learning curves' was first observed by the 19th Century German psychologist Hermann Ebbinghaus according to the difficulty of memorizing varying numbers of verbal stimuli, and subsequent learning about the complex processes of learning are discussed in the

.

The rule used for representing the learning curve effect states that the more times a task has been performed, the less time will be required on each subsequent iteration.

a. Point biserial correlation coefficient
b. Spatial Decision Support Systems
c. Distribution
d. Models

3. _____ is the mathematical study of waiting lines (or queues.) The theory enables mathematical analysis of several related processes, including arriving at the (back of the) queue, waiting in the queue (essentially a storage process), and being served by the server(s) at the front of the queue. The theory permits the derivation and calculation of several performance measures including the average waiting time in the queue or the system, the expected number waiting or receiving service and the probability of encountering the system in certain states, such as empty, full, having an available server or having to wait a certain time to be served.

a. Semimartingale
b. Queueing theory
c. Queueing model
d. Mixing time

4. In statistics, _____ is:

- the arithmetic _____
- the expected value of a random variable, which is also called the population _____.

Chapter 14. Queueing Models

It is sometimes stated that the '_____' _____s average. This is incorrect if '_____' is taken in the specific sense of 'arithmetic _____' as there are different types of averages: the _____, median, and mode. Other simple statistical analyses use measures of spread, such as range, interquartile range, or standard deviation. For a real-valued random variable X, the _____ is the expectation of X. Note that not every probability distribution has a defined _____; see the Cauchy distribution for an example.

a. Statistical inference
b. Correlation
c. Control chart
d. Mean

5. _____ is a way of expressing knowledge or belief that an event will occur or has occurred. In mathematics the concept has been given an exact meaning in _____ theory, that is used extensively in such areas of study as mathematics, statistics, finance, gambling, science, and philosophy to draw conclusions about the likelihood of potential events and the underlying mechanics of complex systems.

The word _____ does not have a consistent direct definition.

a. Statistics
b. Time series analysis
c. Standard deviation
d. Probability

6. In probability theory and statistics, a _____ identifies either the probability of each value of an unidentified random variable (when the variable is discrete), or the probability of the value falling within a particular interval (when the variable is continuous.) The _____ describes the range of possible values that a random variable can attain and the probability that the value of the random variable is within any (measurable) subset of that range. The Normal distribution, often called the 'bell curve'

When the random variable takes values in the set of real numbers, the _____ is completely described by the cumulative distribution function, whose value at each real x is the probability that the random variable is smaller than or equal to x.

a. Probability distribution
b. Frequency distribution
c. Median
d. Statistically significant

Chapter 14. Queueing Models

7. _____ is one of the four elements of marketing mix. An organization or set of organizations (go-betweens) involved in the process of making a product or service available for use or consumption by a consumer or business user.

The other three parts of the marketing mix are product, pricing, and promotion.

  a. Missing completely at random
  b. Distribution
  c. Matching theory
  d. Job creation programs

8. In probability theory and statistics, the _____s are a class of continuous probability distributions. They describe the times between events in a Poisson process, i.e. a process in which events occur continuously and independently at a constant average rate.

The probability density function (pdf) of an _____ is

Here $>\lambda > 0$ is the parameter of the distribution, often called the rate parameter.

  a. A Stake in the Outcome
  b. A4e
  c. AAAI
  d. Exponential distribution

9. _____ is the provision of service to customers before, during and after a purchase.

According to Turban et al. (2002), '_____ is a series of activities designed to enhance the level of customer satisfaction - that is, the feeling that a product or service has met the customer expectation.'

Its importance varies by product, industry and customer; defective or broken merchandise can be exchanged, often only with a receipt and within a specified time frame.

  a. Customer service
  b. Service rate
  c. 28-hour day
  d. 1990 Clean Air Act

Chapter 14. Queueing Models

10. _____ is a service policy where by the requests of customers or clients are attended to in the order that they arrived, without other biases or preferences. The policy can be employed when processing sales orders, in determining restaurant seating, or on a taxi stand, for example.

Festival seating (also known as general seating and stadium seating) is seating done on a FCFS basis.

  a. 28-hour day
  b. 1990 Clean Air Act
  c. 33 Strategies of War
  d. First-come, first-served

11. A _____ is a mathematical model for the random evolution of a memoryless system, that is, one for which the likelihood of a given future state, at any given moment, depends only on its present state, and not on any past states.

In a common description, a stochastic process with the Markov property, or memorylessness, is one for which conditional on the present state of the system, its future and past are independent.

Often, the term Markov chain is used to mean a _____ which has a discrete state-space.

  a. Queueing theory
  b. Mixing time
  c. Stopping time
  d. Markov process

12. A sample is a subject chosen from a population for investigation. A _____ is one chosen by a method involving an unpredictable component. Random sampling can also refer to taking a number of independent observations from the same probability distribution, without involving any real population.
  a. 1990 Clean Air Act
  b. Random sample
  c. 33 Strategies of War
  d. 28-hour day

13. _____ plant, and equipment, is a term used in accountancy for assets and property which cannot easily be converted into cash. This can be compared with current assets such as cash or bank accounts, which are described as liquid assets. In most cases, only tangible assets are referred to as fixed.

a. 28-hour day
b. 33 Strategies of War
c. 1990 Clean Air Act
d. Fixed asset

14. _____ is an advertisement in which a particular product specifically mentions a competitor by name for the express purpose of showing why the competitor is inferior to the product naming it.

This should not be confused with parody advertisements, where a fictional product is being advertised for the purpose of poking fun at the particular advertisement, nor should it be confused with the use of a coined brand name for the purpose of comparing the product without actually naming an actual competitor. ('Wikipedia tastes better and is less filling than the Encyclopedia Galactica.')

In the 1980s, during what has been referred to as the cola wars, soft-drink manufacturer Pepsi ran a series of advertisements where people, caught on hidden camera, in a blind taste test, chose Pepsi over rival Coca-Cola.

a. 33 Strategies of War
b. 1990 Clean Air Act
c. Comparative advertising
d. 28-hour day

15. In business, _____ is a performance metric used to measure the customer service in a supply organization. One example of a _____ measures the number of units filled as a percentage of the total ordered and is known as fill rate. If customer orders total 1000 units, and you can only meet 900 units of that order, your fill rate is 90%.

- In statistics, notably in queuing theory, _____ denotes the rate at which customers are being served in a system. It is the reciprocal of the service time. For example, a supermarket cash desk with an average service time of 30 seconds per customer would have an average _____ of 2 per minute. In statistics the greek letter >μ is used for the _____.

a. Customer service
b. 1990 Clean Air Act
c. 28-hour day
d. Service rate

16. In probability theory and statistics, the _____ of a random variable is the integral of the random variable with respect to its probability measure. For discrete random variables this is equivalent to the probability-weighted sum of the possible values, and for continuous random variables with a density function it is the probability density -weighted integral of the possible values.

Chapter 14. Queueing Models

a. AAAI
b. Expected value
c. A Stake in the Outcome
d. A4e

17. In queueing theory, _____ is the proportion of the system's resources which is used by the traffic which arrives at it. It should be strictly less than one for the system to function well. It is usually represented by the symbol ρ.

a. AAAI
b. A Stake in the Outcome
c. A4e
d. Utilization

18. The method of _____ is used to approximately solve overdetermined systems, i.e. systems of equations in which there are more equations than unknowns. _____ is often applied in statistical contexts, particularly regression analysis.

_____ can be interpreted as a method of fitting data.

a. Stepwise regression
b. Trend analysis
c. Regression analysis
d. Least squares

19. In economics, business, retail, and accounting, a _____ is the value of money that has been used up to produce something, and hence is not available for use anymore. In economics, a _____ is an alternative that is given up as a result of a decision. In business, the _____ may be one of acquisition, in which case the amount of money expended to acquire it is counted as _____.

a. Fixed costs
b. Cost overrun
c. Cost allocation
d. Cost

20. _____ refers to metrics and measures of output from production processes, per unit of input. Labor _____, for example, is typically measured as a ratio of output per labor-hour, an input. _____ may be conceived of as a metrics of the technical or engineering efficiency of production.

a. Value engineering
b. Master production schedule
c. Remanufacturing
d. Productivity

21. _____, is the discipline of using scientific research-based principles, strategies, and other analytical methods, such as mathematical modeling to improve any organization's ability to enact rational, meaningful business management decisions.
   a. Trustee
   b. Workflow
   c. Cross ownership
   d. Management Science

Chapter 15. Computer Simulation: Basic Concepts

1. _____ is one of the four elements of marketing mix. An organization or set of organizations (go-betweens) involved in the process of making a product or service available for use or consumption by a consumer or business user.

The other three parts of the marketing mix are product, pricing, and promotion.

   a. Missing completely at random
   b. Distribution
   c. Matching theory
   d. Job creation programs

2. The function f is called, variously, an _____, cost function, energy function, or energy functional. A feasible solution that minimizes (or maximizes, if that is the goal) the _____ is called an optimal solution.

Generally, when the feasible region or the _____ of the problem does not present convexity, there may be several local minima and maxima, where a local minimum x^* is defined as a point for which there exists some $>\delta > 0$ so that for all x such that

the expression

holds; that is to say, on some region around x^* all of the function values are greater than or equal to the value at that point.

   a. A4e
   b. A Stake in the Outcome
   c. AAAI
   d. Objective function

3. _____ has the following meanings:

The care and servicing by personnel for the purpose of maintaining equipment and facilities in satisfactory operating condition by providing for systematic inspection, detection, and correction of incipient failures either before they occur or before they develop into major defects.

   1. Maintenance, including tests, measurements, adjustments, and parts replacement, performed specifically to prevent faults from occurring.

While _____ is generally considered to be worthwhile, there are risks such as equipment failure or human error involved when performing _____, just as in any maintenance operation. _____ as scheduled overhaul or scheduled replacement provides two of the three proactive failure management policies available to the maintenance engineer. Common methods of determining what _____ failure management policies should be applied are; OEM recommendations, requirements of codes and legislation within a jurisdiction, what an 'expert' thinks ought to be done, or the maintenance that's already done to similar equipment.

   a. 28-hour day
   b. 33 Strategies of War
   c. 1990 Clean Air Act
   d. Preventive maintenance

4. In probability theory, a probability distribution is called _____ if its cumulative distribution function is _____. This is equivalent to saying that for random variables X with the distribution in question, Pr[X = a] = 0 for all real numbers a, i.e.: the probability that X attains the value a is zero, for any number a. If the distribution of X is _____ then X is called a _____ random variable.
   a. Decision tree pruning
   b. Continuous
   c. Connectionist expert systems
   d. Pay Band

5. In probability theory and statistics, a _____ identifies either the probability of each value of an unidentified random variable (when the variable is discrete), or the probability of the value falling within a particular interval (when the variable is continuous.) The _____ describes the range of possible values that a random variable can attain and the probability that the value of the random variable is within any (measurable) subset of that range. The Normal distribution, often called the 'bell curve'

When the random variable takes values in the set of real numbers, the _____ is completely described by the cumulative distribution function, whose value at each real x is the probability that the random variable is smaller than or equal to x.

   a. Median
   b. Frequency distribution
   c. Statistically significant
   d. Probability distribution

6. In probability theory and statistics, the _____ or just distribution function, completely describes the probability distribution of a real-valued random variable X. For every real number x, the _____ of X is given by

where the right-hand side represents the probability that the random variable X takes on a value less than or equal to x. The probability that X lies in the interval (a, b] is therefore $F_X(b) >- F_X(a)$ if a < b.

If treating several random variables X, Y, ...

a. Cumulative distribution function
b. 33 Strategies of War
c. 1990 Clean Air Act
d. 28-hour day

7. _____ is a way of expressing knowledge or belief that an event will occur or has occurred. In mathematics the concept has been given an exact meaning in _____ theory, that is used extensively in such areas of study as mathematics, statistics, finance, gambling, science, and philosophy to draw conclusions about the likelihood of potential events and the underlying mechanics of complex systems.

The word _____ does not have a consistent direct definition.

a. Time series analysis
b. Statistics
c. Probability
d. Standard deviation

8. In probability theory and statistics, the _____ or Gaussian distribution is a continuous probability distribution that describes data that clusters around a mean or average. The graph of the associated probability density function is bell-shaped, with a peak at the mean, and is known as the Gaussian function or bell curve.

The _____ can be used to describe, at least approximately, any variable that tends to cluster around the mean.

a. Normal distribution
b. Generalized normal distribution
c. Heteroskedastic
d. Histogram

Chapter 15. Computer Simulation: Basic Concepts

9. In probability theory and statistics, the _____s are a class of continuous probability distributions. They describe the times between events in a Poisson process, i.e. a process in which events occur continuously and independently at a constant average rate.

The probability density function (pdf) of an _____ is

$$$$

Here $>\lambda > 0$ is the parameter of the distribution, often called the rate parameter.

   a. AAAI
   b. A4e
   c. A Stake in the Outcome
   d. Exponential distribution

10. A _____ is one of several ways of doing research whether it is social science related or even socially related. It is an intensive study of a single group, incident, or community. Other ways include experiments, surveys, multiple histories, and analysis of archival information.

Rather than using samples and following a rigid protocol to examine limited number of variables, _____ methods involve an in-depth, longitudinal examination of a single instance or event: a case.

   a. Case study
   b. Longitudinal study
   c. 1990 Clean Air Act
   d. Standard operating procedure

11. In statistics, a _____ is an interval estimate of a population parameter. Instead of estimating the parameter by a single value, an interval likely to include the parameter is given. Thus, _____s are used to indicate the reliability of an estimate.
   a. Confidence interval
   b. Statistically significant
   c. Histogram
   d. Simple moving average

12. The method of _____ is used to approximately solve overdetermined systems, i.e. systems of equations in which there are more equations than unknowns. _____ is often applied in statistical contexts, particularly regression analysis.

_____ can be interpreted as a method of fitting data.

a. Stepwise regression
b. Regression analysis
c. Trend analysis
d. Least squares

13. In queueing theory, a _____ is used to approximate a real queueing situation or system, so the queueing behaviour can be analysed mathematically. _____s allow a number of useful steady state performance measures to be determined, including:

- the average number in the queue, or the system,
- the average time spent in the queue, or the system,
- the statistical distribution of those numbers or times,
- the probability the queue is full, or empty, and
- the probability of finding the system in a particular state.

These performance measures are important as issues or problems caused by queueing situations are often related to customer dissatisfaction with service or may be the root cause of economic losses in a business. Analysis of the relevant _____s allows the cause of queueing issues to be identified and the impact of proposed changes to be assessed.

Queuing models can be represented using Kendall's notation:

   A/B/S/K/N/Disc

where:

- A is the interarrival time distribution
- B is the service time distribution
- S is the number of servers
- K is the system capacity
- N is the calling population
- Disc is the service discipline assumed

Many times the last members are omitted, so the notation becomes A/B/S and it is assumed that K = ∞, N = ∞ and Disc = FIFO.

Chapter 15. Computer Simulation: Basic Concepts

Some standard notation for distributions (A or B) are:

- M for a Markovian (exponential) distribution
- E>κ for an Erlang distribution with >κ phases
- D for Degenerate (or Deterministic) distribution (constant)
- G for General distribution (arbitrary)
- PH for a Phase-type distribution

_____s are generally constructed to represent the steady state of a queueing system, that is, the typical, long run or average state of the system. As a consequence, these are stochastic models that represent the probability that a queueing system will be found in a particular configuration or state.

a. Queueing theory
b. Girsanov theorem
c. Markov process
d. Queueing model

14. The term _____ in logic applies to arguments or statements.

An argument is valid if and only if the truth of its premises entails the truth of its conclusion, it would be self-contradictory to affirm the premises and deny the conclusion. The corresponding conditional of a valid argument is a logical truth and the negation of its corresponding conditional is a contradiction.

a. Fuzzy logic
b. Validity
c. 1990 Clean Air Act
d. Simplification

15. The Program (or Project) Evaluation and Review Technique, commonly abbreviated _____, is a model for project management designed to analyze and represent the tasks involved in completing a given project.

_____ is a method to analyze the involved tasks in completing a given project, specially the time needed to complete each task, and identifying the minimum time needed to complete the total project.

_____ was developed primarily to simplify the planning and scheduling of large and complex projects.

Chapter 15. Computer Simulation: Basic Concepts

a. 33 Strategies of War
b. 1990 Clean Air Act
c. 28-hour day
d. PERT

16. _____ refers to the movement of cash into or out of a business or financial product. It is usually measured during a specified, finite period of time. Measurement of _____ can be used

- to determine a project's rate of return or value. The time of _____s into and out of projects are used as inputs in financial models such as internal rate of return, and net present value.
- to determine problems with a business's liquidity. Being profitable does not necessarily mean being liquid. A company can fail because of a shortage of cash, even while profitable.
- as an alternate measure of a business's profits when it is believed that accrual accounting concepts do not represent economic realities. For example, a company may be notionally profitable but generating little operational cash (as may be the case for a company that barters its products rather than selling for cash.) In such a case, the company may be deriving additional operating cash by issuing shares evaluating default risk, re-investment requirements, etc.

_____ is a generic term used differently depending on the context. It may be defined by users for their own purposes.

a. Gross profit margin
b. Sweat equity
c. Gross profit
d. Cash flow

17. _____ is the use of control systems (such as numerical control, programmable logic control, and other industrial control systems), in concert with other applications of information technology (such as computer-aided technologies [CAD, CAM, CAx]), to control industrial machinery and processes, reducing the need for human intervention. In the scope of industrialization, _____ is a step beyond mechanization. Whereas mechanization provided human operators with machinery to assist them with the physical requirements of work, _____ greatly reduces the need for human sensory and mental requirements as well.

a. AAAI
b. A4e
c. A Stake in the Outcome
d. Automation

18. _____ is normally any risk associated with any form of financing. Risk is probability of unfavorable condition; in financial sector it is the probability of actual return being less than expected return. There will be uncertainty in every business; the level of uncertainty present is called risk.

a. Financial risk
b. Long term investment plan
c. Choquet integral
d. Holding cost

19. _____ is an advertisement in which a particular product specifically mentions a competitor by name for the express purpose of showing why the competitor is inferior to the product naming it.

This should not be confused with parody advertisements, where a fictional product is being advertised for the purpose of poking fun at the particular advertisement, nor should it be confused with the use of a coined brand name for the purpose of comparing the product without actually naming an actual competitor. ('Wikipedia tastes better and is less filling than the Encyclopedia Galactica.')

In the 1980s, during what has been referred to as the cola wars, soft-drink manufacturer Pepsi ran a series of advertisements where people, caught on hidden camera, in a blind taste test, chose Pepsi over rival Coca-Cola.

a. 1990 Clean Air Act
b. 33 Strategies of War
c. 28-hour day
d. Comparative advertising

20. In decision theory and estimation theory, the _____ of an estimator, $\hat{\theta}$, of an unknown parameter of the distribution, θ, is the expected value of the loss function

$$R(\theta, \hat{\theta}) = \mathbb{E}_\theta L(\theta, \hat{\theta}) = \int L(\theta, \hat{\theta}) \, dP_\theta.$$

where dP_θ is a probability measure parametrized by θ.

- For a scalar parameter θ and a quadratic loss function,

$$L(\theta, \hat{\theta}) = (\theta - \hat{\theta})^2$$

the _____ function becomes the mean squared error of the estimate,

$$R(\theta, \hat{\theta}) = E_\theta (\theta - \hat{\theta})^2$$

- In density estimation, the unknown parameter is probability density itself. The loss function is typically chosen to be a norm in an appropriate function space. For example, for L^2 norm,

$$L(f, \hat{f}) = \|f - \hat{f}\|_2^2$$

the _____ function becomes the mean integrated squared error

$$R(f, \hat{f}) = E\|f - \hat{f}\|^2$$

a. Linear model
b. Risk aversion
c. Financial modeling
d. Risk

21. _____, is the discipline of using scientific research-based principles, strategies, and other analytical methods, such as mathematical modeling to improve any organization's ability to enact rational, meaningful business management decisions.
   a. Workflow
   b. Cross ownership
   c. Trustee
   d. Management science

22. A _____ is the period of time between the initiation of any process of production and the completion of that process. Thus the _____ for ordering a new car from a manufacturer may be anywhere from 2 weeks to 6 months. In industry, _____ reduction is an important part of lean manufacturing.

Chapter 15. Computer Simulation: Basic Concepts

a. 1990 Clean Air Act
b. 33 Strategies of War
c. 28-hour day
d. Lead time

23. A _____ is a graph (flow chart) depicting the sequence in which a project's terminal elements are to be completed by showing terminal elements and their dependencies.

The work breakdown structure or the product breakdown structure show the 'part-whole' relations. In contrast, the _____ shows the 'before-after' relations.

a. 28-hour day
b. 1990 Clean Air Act
c. 33 Strategies of War
d. Project network

1. The _____ model is a mathematical model in operations management and applied economics used to determine optimal inventory levels. It is (typically) characterized by fixed prices and uncertain demand. If the inventory level is q, each unit of demand above q is lost.

The standard _____ profit function is:

where D is a random variable representing demand, each unit is sold for price p and purchased for price c, and E is the expectation operator. The solution to the optimal stocking quantity of the _____ is:

where F^{-1} denotes the inverse cumulative distribution function of D.

   a. Multiscale decision making
   b. 28-hour day
   c. 1990 Clean Air Act
   d. Newsvendor

2. In decision theory and estimation theory, the _____ of an estimator, $\hat{\theta}$, of an unknown parameter of the distribution, θ, is the expected value of the loss function

$$R(\theta, \hat{\theta}) = \mathbb{E}_\theta L(\theta, \hat{\theta}) = \int L(\theta, \hat{\theta})\, dP_\theta.$$

where dP_θ is a probability measure parametrized by θ.

- For a scalar parameter θ and a quadratic loss function,

$$L(\theta, \hat{\theta}) = (\theta - \hat{\theta})^2$$

the _____ function becomes the mean squared error of the estimate,

$$R(\theta, \hat{\theta}) = E_\theta(\theta - \hat{\theta})^2$$

- In density estimation, the unknown parameter is probability density itself. The loss function is typically chosen to be a norm in an appropriate function space. For example, for L^2 norm,

$$L(f, \hat{f}) = \|f - \hat{f}\|_2^2$$

the _____ function becomes the mean integrated squared error

$$R(f, \hat{f}) = E\|f - \hat{f}\|^2$$

a. Financial modeling
b. Risk aversion
c. Linear model
d. Risk

3. _____ is one of the four elements of marketing mix. An organization or set of organizations (go-betweens) involved in the process of making a product or service available for use or consumption by a consumer or business user.

The other three parts of the marketing mix are product, pricing, and promotion.

a. Missing completely at random
b. Distribution
c. Job creation programs
d. Matching theory

Chapter 16. Computer Simulation with Crystal Ball
93

4. In finance, an _____ is a contract between a buyer and a seller that gives the buyer the right--but not the obligation-- to buy or to sell a particular asset (the underlying asset) at a later day at an agreed price. In return for granting the _____, the seller collects a payment (the premium) from the buyer. A call _____ gives the buyer the right to buy the underlying asset; a put _____ gives the buyer of the _____ the right to sell the underlying asset.
   a. A4e
   b. AAAI
   c. A Stake in the Outcome
   d. Option

5. In statistics, _____ is:

   - the arithmetic _____
   - the expected value of a random variable, which is also called the population _____.

It is sometimes stated that the '_____' _____s average. This is incorrect if '_____' is taken in the specific sense of 'arithmetic _____' as there are different types of averages: the _____, median, and mode. Other simple statistical analyses use measures of spread, such as range, interquartile range, or standard deviation. For a real-valued random variable X, the _____ is the expectation of X. Note that not every probability distribution has a defined _____; see the Cauchy distribution for an example.

   a. Correlation
   b. Statistical inference
   c. Control chart
   d. Mean

6. In probability theory and statistics, a _____ is described as the number separating the higher half of a sample, a population, or a probability distribution from the lower half. The _____ of a finite list of numbers can be found by arranging all the observations from lowest value to highest value and picking the middle one. If there is an even number of observations, the _____ is not unique, so one often takes the mean of the two middle values.
   a. Probability distribution
   b. Correlation
   c. Confidence interval
   d. Median

7. In statistics, a _____ is an interval estimate of a population parameter. Instead of estimating the parameter by a single value, an interval likely to include the parameter is given. Thus, _____s are used to indicate the reliability of an estimate.

Chapter 16. Computer Simulation with Crystal Ball

   a. Statistically significant
   b. Histogram
   c. Simple moving average
   d. Confidence interval

8. In the fields of science, engineering, industry and statistics, _____ is the degree of closeness of a measured or calculated quantity to its actual (true) value. _____ is closely related to precision, also called reproducibility or repeatability, the degree to which further measurements or calculations show the same or similar results. _____ indicates proximity to the true value, precision to the repeatability or reproducibility of the measurement

The results of calculations or a measurement can be accurate but not precise, precise but not accurate, neither, or both.

   a. Accuracy
   b. AAAI
   c. A Stake in the Outcome
   d. A4e

9. A _____ is one of several ways of doing research whether it is social science related or even socially related. It is an intensive study of a single group, incident, or community. Other ways include experiments, surveys, multiple histories, and analysis of archival information .

Rather than using samples and following a rigid protocol to examine limited number of variables, _____ methods involve an in-depth, longitudinal examination of a single instance or event: a case.

   a. Longitudinal study
   b. 1990 Clean Air Act
   c. Case study
   d. Standard operating procedure

10. _____ refers to the movement of cash into or out of a business or financial product. It is usually measured during a specified, finite period of time. Measurement of _____ can be used

- to determine a project's rate of return or value. The time of _____s into and out of projects are used as inputs in financial models such as internal rate of return, and net present value.
- to determine problems with a business's liquidity. Being profitable does not necessarily mean being liquid. A company can fail because of a shortage of cash, even while profitable.
- as an alternate measure of a business's profits when it is believed that accrual accounting concepts do not represent economic realities. For example, a company may be notionally profitable but generating little operational cash (as may be the case for a company that barters its products rather than selling for cash.) In such a case, the company may be deriving additional operating cash by issuing shares evaluating default risk, re-investment requirements, etc.

_____ is a generic term used differently depending on the context. It may be defined by users for their own purposes.

a. Cash flow
b. Gross profit
c. Sweat equity
d. Gross profit margin

11. _____ is the discipline of planning, organizing and managing resources to bring about the successful completion of specific project goals and objectives. It is often closely related to and sometimes conflated with Program management.

A project is a finite endeavor--having specific start and completion dates--undertaken to meet particular goals and objectives, usually to bring about beneficial change or added value.

a. Precedence diagram
b. Work package
c. Project engineer
d. Project management

12. The Program (or Project) Evaluation and Review Technique, commonly abbreviated _____, is a model for project management designed to analyze and represent the tasks involved in completing a given project.

_____ is a method to analyze the involved tasks in completing a given project, specially the time needed to complete each task, and identifying the minimum time needed to complete the total project.

_____ was developed primarily to simplify the planning and scheduling of large and complex projects.

Chapter 16. Computer Simulation with Crystal Ball

   a. 28-hour day
   b. 1990 Clean Air Act
   c. 33 Strategies of War
   d. PERT

13. _____ is normally any risk associated with any form of financing. Risk is probability of unfavorable condition; in financial sector it is the probability of actual return being less than expected return. There will be uncertainty in every business; the level of uncertainty present is called risk.
   a. Choquet integral
   b. Long term investment plan
   c. Holding cost
   d. Financial risk

14. A _____ shows us a summarized grouping of data divided into mutually exclusive classes and the number of occurrences in a class. It is a way of showing unorganized data e.g. to show results of an election, income of people for a certain region, sales of a product within a certain period, student loan amounts of graduates, etc. Some of the graphs that can be used with _____s are histograms, line graphs, bar charts and pie charts.
   a. Homoscedastic
   b. Statistics
   c. Frequency distribution
   d. Statistically significant

15. _____ or net present worth (NPW) is defined as the total present value (PV) of a time series of cash flows. It is a standard method for using the time value of money to appraise long-term projects. Used for capital budgeting, and widely throughout economics, it measures the excess or shortfall of cash flows, in present value terms, once financing charges are met.
   a. 1990 Clean Air Act
   b. Discounted cash flow
   c. Present value
   d. Net present value

16. _____ is the value on a given date of a future payment or series of future payments, discounted to reflect the time value of money and other factors such as investment risk. _____ calculations are widely used in business and economics to provide a means to compare cash flows at different times on a meaningful 'like to like' basis.

If offered a choice between $100 today or $100 in one year, everyone will choose $100 today.

a. Present value
b. Discounted cash flow
c. 1990 Clean Air Act
d. Net present value

17. The _____ is an interest rate a central bank charges depository institutions that borrow reserves from it.

The term _____ has two meanings:

- the same as interest rate; the term 'discount' does not refer to the meaning of the word, but to the purpose of using the quantity, such as computations of present value, e.g. net present value or discounted cash flow

- the annual effective _____, which is the annual interest divided by the capital including that interest; this rate is lower than the interest rate; it corresponds to using the value after a year as the nominal value, and seeing the initial value as the nominal value minus a discount; it is used for Treasury Bills and similar financial instruments

The annual effective _____ is the annual interest divided by the capital including that interest, which is the interest rate divided by 100% plus the interest rate. It is the annual discount factor to be applied to the future cash flow, to find the discount, subtracted from a future value to find the value one year earlier.

For example, suppose there is a government bond that sells for $95 and pays $100 in a year's time.

a. Discount rate
b. 1990 Clean Air Act
c. 33 Strategies of War
d. 28-hour day

18. The _____ of an edge is $c_f(u, v) = c(u, v) - f(u, v)$. This defines a residual network denoted $G_f(V, E_f)$, giving the amount of available capacity. See that there can be an edge from u to v in the residual network, even though there is no edge from u to v in the original network.

a. 28-hour day
b. 33 Strategies of War
c. 1990 Clean Air Act
d. Residual capacity

19. _____, is the discipline of using scientific research-based principles, strategies, and other analytical methods, such as mathematical modeling to improve any organization's ability to enact rational, meaningful business management decisions.

Chapter 16. Computer Simulation with Crystal Ball

   a. Trustee
   b. Workflow
   c. Cross ownership
   d. Management Science

20. _____ is the process of understanding, anticipating and influencing consumer behavior in order to maximize revenue or profits from a fixed, perishable resource This process was first discovered by Dr. Matt H. Keller. The challenge is to sell the right resources to the right customer at the right time for the right price.
   a. Business model design
   b. Yield management
   c. Business networking
   d. Gap analysis

21. In probability theory and statistics, the _____ or Gaussian distribution is a continuous probability distribution that describes data that clusters around a mean or average. The graph of the associated probability density function is bell-shaped, with a peak at the mean, and is known as the Gaussian function or bell curve.

The _____ can be used to describe, at least approximately, any variable that tends to cluster around the mean.

   a. Normal distribution
   b. Histogram
   c. Generalized normal distribution
   d. Heteroskedastic

22. In probability theory and statistics, the _____ is the discrete probability distribution of the number of successes in a sequence of n independent yes/no experiments, each of which yields success with probability p. Such a success/failure experiment is also called a Bernoulli experiment or Bernoulli trial. In fact, when n = 1, the _____ is a Bernoulli distribution.
   a. Probability
   b. Binomial distribution
   c. Statistics
   d. Discrete probability distributions

23. In probability theory, a probability distribution is called _____ if its cumulative distribution function is _____. This is equivalent to saying that for random variables X with the distribution in question, Pr[X = a] = 0 for all real numbers a, i.e.: the probability that X attains the value a is zero, for any number a. If the distribution of X is _____ then X is called a _____ random variable.

a. Continuous
b. Pay Band
c. Connectionist expert systems
d. Decision tree pruning

24. In probability theory and statistics, a _____ identifies either the probability of each value of an unidentified random variable (when the variable is discrete), or the probability of the value falling within a particular interval (when the variable is continuous.) The _____ describes the range of possible values that a random variable can attain and the probability that the value of the random variable is within any (measurable) subset of that range. The Normal distribution, often called the 'bell curve'

When the random variable takes values in the set of real numbers, the _____ is completely described by the cumulative distribution function, whose value at each real x is the probability that the random variable is smaller than or equal to x.

a. Statistically significant
b. Probability distribution
c. Median
d. Frequency distribution

25. _____ is a way of expressing knowledge or belief that an event will occur or has occurred. In mathematics the concept has been given an exact meaning in _____ theory, that is used extensively in such areas of study as mathematics, statistics, finance, gambling, science, and philosophy to draw conclusions about the likelihood of potential events and the underlying mechanics of complex systems.

The word _____ does not have a consistent direct definition.

a. Time series analysis
b. Statistics
c. Standard deviation
d. Probability

26. The _____ for the normal distribution is given by

$$f(x;\mu,\sigma) = \frac{1}{\sigma\sqrt{2\pi}} \exp\left(-\frac{(x-\mu)^2}{2\sigma^2}\right),$$

where μ is the mean and σ the standard deviation.

By the definition of a _____, f must integrate to 1. That is,

$$I = \int_{-\infty}^{\infty} f(x)\,dx = 1.$$

However, this integration is not straight-forward, since f does not have an antiderivative in closed form.

a. Law of total expectation
b. Probability density function
c. Conditional expectation
d. Fano factor

27. In probability theory and statistics, the _____ is a continuous probability distribution with lower limit a, mode c and upper limit b.

The distribution simplifies when c = a or c = b. For example, if a = 0, b = 1 and c = 1, then the equations above become:

This distribution for a = 0, b = 1 and c = 0.5 is distribution of X = $(X_1 + X_2)/2$, where X_1, X_2 are two independent random variables with standard uniform distribution.

a. 28-hour day
b. 33 Strategies of War
c. 1990 Clean Air Act
d. Triangular distribution

28. In probability theory and statistics, the _____ is a continuous probability distribution. It is named after Waloddi Weibull who described it in detail in 1951, although it was first identified by Fr>échet (1927) and first applied by Rosin ' Rammler (1933) to describe the size distribution of particles. The probability density function of a Weibull random variable x is:

where k > 0 is the shape parameter and >λ > 0 is the scale parameter of the distribution.

a. 28-hour day
b. Weibull distribution
c. 33 Strategies of War
d. 1990 Clean Air Act

29. In probability theory and statistics, the _____s are a class of continuous probability distributions. They describe the times between events in a Poisson process, i.e. a process in which events occur continuously and independently at a constant average rate.

The probability density function (pdf) of an _____ is

Here >λ > 0 is the parameter of the distribution, often called the rate parameter.

a. Exponential distribution
b. AAAI
c. A4e
d. A Stake in the Outcome

30. In probability and statistics the _____ is a discrete probability distribution. It arises as the probability distribution of the number of failures in a sequence of Bernoulli trials needed to get a specified (non-random) number of successes. If one throws a die repeatedly until the third time a '1' appears, then the probability distribution of the number of non-'1's that appear before the third '1' is a _____.
a. 28-hour day
b. 33 Strategies of War
c. 1990 Clean Air Act
d. Negative binomial distribution

31. In economics, _____ is the desire to own something and the ability to pay for it. The term _____ signifies the ability or the willingness to buy a particular commodity at a given point of time.

a. Demand
b. 33 Strategies of War
c. 1990 Clean Air Act
d. 28-hour day

32. _____ can be regarded as an outcome of mental processes (cognitive process) leading to the selection of a course of action among several alternatives. Every _____ process produces a final choice. The output can be an action or an opinion of choice.
   a. 1990 Clean Air Act
   b. 33 Strategies of War
   c. 28-hour day
   d. Decision making

33. _____ is one of the four Ps of the marketing mix. The other three aspects are product, promotion, and place. It is also a key variable in microeconomic price allocation theory.
   a. Penetration pricing
   b. Price floor
   c. Pricing
   d. Transfer pricing

34. In economics, business, retail, and accounting, a _____ is the value of money that has been used up to produce something, and hence is not available for use anymore. In economics, a _____ is an alternative that is given up as a result of a decision. In business, the _____ may be one of acquisition, in which case the amount of money expended to acquire it is counted as _____.
   a. Fixed costs
   b. Cost
   c. Cost overrun
   d. Cost allocation

35. In mathematics, _____ are used in the study of chance and probability. They were developed to assist in the analysis of games of chance, stochastic events, and the results of scientific experiments by capturing only the mathematical properties necessary to answer probabilistic questions. Further formalizations have firmly grounded the entity in the theoretical domains of mathematics by making use of measure theory.

a. Median
b. Correlation
c. Time series
d. Random variables

Chapter 1
| 1. a | 2. c | 3. d | 4. d | 5. b | 6. b | 7. b | 8. c | 9. c | 10. d |
| 11. d | 12. d | 13. d | 14. d | 15. b | 16. d | 17. a | 18. d | 19. b | 20. c |

Chapter 2
1. c	2. a	3. b	4. d	5. a	6. b	7. d	8. b	9. b	10. b
11. d	12. c	13. d	14. b	15. d	16. d	17. d	18. d	19. a	20. d
21. d	22. a	23. c							

Chapter 3
| 1. a | 2. a | 3. a | 4. d | 5. c |

Chapter 4
| 1. b | 2. d | 3. d | 4. d | 5. d | 6. b | 7. b | 8. d | 9. d | 10. d |
| 11. a | 12. d | 13. c | | | | | | | |

Chapter 5
| 1. d | 2. c | 3. a | 4. c | 5. c | 6. d | 7. d | 8. d |

Chapter 6
| 1. d | 2. c | 3. d | 4. c | 5. d | 6. d | 7. d | 8. d | 9. d | 10. d |
| 11. d | 12. d | 13. b | 14. b | | | | | | |

Chapter 7
| 1. a | 2. d | 3. a | 4. d | 5. d | 6. b | 7. d | 8. d |

Chapter 8
1. b	2. a	3. a	4. d	5. d	6. d	7. a	8. d	9. d	10. d
11. b	12. a	13. d	14. d	15. c	16. a	17. d	18. b	19. d	20. d
21. d	22. d								

Chapter 9
| 1. b | 2. c | 3. d | 4. b | 5. d | 6. d | 7. d | 8. b | 9. d | 10. c |
| 11. b | 12. c | | | | | | | | |

Chapter 10
| 1. c | 2. d | 3. d | 4. d | 5. d | 6. d | 7. d | 8. d | 9. d | 10. d |
| 11. c | 12. c | 13. a | 14. b | 15. d | | | | | |

Chapter 11
| 1. b | 2. d | 3. b | 4. c |

Chapter 12
1. d	2. d	3. c	4. c	5. a	6. a	7. a	8. a	9. d	10. c
11. d	12. d	13. b	14. d	15. a	16. d	17. d	18. c	19. d	20. d
21. a	22. d	23. d	24. d						

ANSWER KEY

Chapter 13
1. a	2. d	3. c	4. a	5. d	6. b	7. d	8. b	9. c	10. a
11. a	12. d	13. d	14. d	15. d	16. d	17. b	18. c	19. b	20. c
21. d	22. a	23. b	24. c	25. d	26. d				

Chapter 14
1. a	2. d	3. b	4. d	5. d	6. a	7. b	8. d	9. a	10. d
11. d	12. b	13. d	14. c	15. d	16. b	17. d	18. d	19. d	20. d
21. d									

Chapter 15
1. b	2. d	3. d	4. b	5. d	6. a	7. c	8. a	9. d	10. a
11. a	12. d	13. d	14. b	15. d	16. d	17. d	18. a	19. d	20. d
21. d	22. d	23. d							

Chapter 16
1. d	2. d	3. b	4. d	5. d	6. d	7. d	8. a	9. c	10. a
11. d	12. d	13. d	14. c	15. d	16. a	17. a	18. d	19. d	20. b
21. a	22. b	23. a	24. b	25. d	26. b	27. d	28. b	29. a	30. d
31. a	32. d	33. c	34. b	35. d					

www.ingramcontent.com/pod-product-compliance
Lightning Source LLC
Chambersburg PA
CBHW081204240426
43669CB00039B/2808